Advance Praise for The Absolute Woman

"Vicky Tiel has inspired generations of women around the globe. She has the unique ability to empower women and give them the confidence gained through the combination of femininity and strength. *The Absolute Woman* will become an important companion for women who are looking to be inspired and bring out the femininity and power in themselves."—Mindy Grossman, CEO, Weight Watchers International

"Vicky 'absolutely' understands a woman's Mind, Body and Spirit. I love her ten points for Feminine Power, as well as her wise and wonderful guidance for dressing, working, eating and creating."—Amy Zerner, artist, designer, bestselling author

"Vicky Tiel has done it again! Her first book, *It's All About the Dress*, was an absolute must read for anyone even remotely interested in fashion. And years later, Vicky apparently has more to say. In her latest book, *The Absolute Woman*, Vicky teaches women how to succeed in business without compromising their femininity, and she is living proof of how it's done. Way before #TimesUp and the #MeTooMovement, Vicky Tiel was blazing the trail for generations of women to come. In her new book, Vicky explains how she went from a young fashion student upstart, to one of the top Paris designers, and then how she went on to craft a successful fragrance empire. This book will inspire and empower girls everywhere, from Baby Boomers to iGens."—Francesca Sterlacci, Founder, University of Fashion

"Vicky Tiel, through decades of beautifully dressing women from the famous to the infamous, knows practically everything there is to know about Femininity and Power. In her new book, *The Absolute Woman*, she will show you how to unlock that power within you!" — Jeffrey Banks, Coty Award-winning fashion designer, author

Vicky Tiel
Vicky Tiel
Vicky Tiel
Vicky Tiel
Vicky Tiel
Vicky Tiel
Vicky Tiel
Vicky Tiel

the Absolute Woman

IT'S ALL ABOUT FEMININE POWER

VICKY TIEL

Post Hill
PRESS

Girlfriends Talk

Vicky Tiel

This book is dedicated to my girlfriends who made me write Book Two after Sassy, my beloved German Shepherd, suddenly died.

Mary Alice Orito, artist and life coach.

Mia Fonssagrives Solow, ex-partner and forever friend.

My dear young neighbors, Julie Shumway from our Florida farm and Ashley from the upstate New York mountain cabin who helped me with my book.

Dusty Simi and Joan Ritter, my "road trip" girlfriends.

Delisa Beamon, Alma Vidovic, and Amber Clark, my precious thirty-year-olds who keep me young.

Catherine Russell and Dora Gaffaney, my dearest perfume ladies.

Bonnie Nadell, my Hollywood agent, thank you.

A POST HILL PRESS BOOK

The Absolute Woman:
It's All About Feminine Power
© 2018 by Vicky Tiel
All Rights Reserved

ISBN: 978-1-64293-009-2
ISBN (eBook): 978-1-64293-010-8

Cover art by Cody Corcoran
Cover photo by Ron Berkeley
Interior Design and Composition by Greg Johnson/Textbook Perfect

Post Hill Press
New York • Nashville
posthillpress.com

Published in the United States of America

Contents

The Absolute Woman

IT'S ALL ABOUT FEMININE POWER

Vicky Tiel

Introduction

I've been a nobody and I've been a somebody. I've met and worked with some of the most famous people in the world and I've had a great time living and being with people that nobody knows.

I was married for years to a man fifteen years older, a "Hollywood" husband, who cheated on me with every beautiful woman who sat in his makeup chair. Now I have a Florida fisherman husband, fifteen years younger, who has loved me for thirty years.

Today I am the longest lasting female fashion designer in Paris, France. I've sold the same couture dress (the "Pretty Woman") in Bergdorf Goodman and Neiman Marcus for thirty-two straight years, breaking their continuous sales record.

Here in *The Absolute Woman* is everything that I've learned in my fifty-three years in fashion and beauty from the world's greatest actresses, top models, and the powerful wives of the most powerful men in the world. I've dressed the entire court of Farah Diba Pahlavi (the wife of the Shah of Iran), designed the wedding gowns of Mrs. Gotti and Miss Gambino of New York and the inaugural gown of Jill Biden, and dressed two Mrs. Trumps. I've even dressed Oprah in my purple "Pretty Woman" dress for the cover of O magazine.

The biggest question for women today is "What do we need to do to make ourselves FEEL POWERFUL and BE POWERFUL?"

I hope to answer this question.

I hope to teach women to make the right life decisions.

Elizabeth Taylor

1964

"We are not a product of our circumstances, we are a product of our decisions."

BOB CIRCOSTA
(HELPED CREATE THE TV SHOPPING INDUSTRY)

A Change in My Life: Two Things

Two things happened just before my first book came out that changed my life.

The first tragedy was the murder of a very dear friend. It was November 2010. I was on a bus going to Washington D.C. from New York City to appear at Neiman Marcus in Chevy Chase, Maryland, my home town. I was about to telephone Ronni Chasen, a Hollywood publicist who had recently rented an apartment in Paris on Rue des Beaux-Arts, a block away from my shop on 21 Rue Bonaparte. We were scheduled to meet in Paris the following week. Just as I was about to call, I glanced down at the newspaper on my lap and saw on the cover of the *New York Post* that Ronni Chasen had been gunned down in her car in Beverly Hills the night before, after previewing a movie she was promoting with Cher.

I screamed "Oh my God" so loudly on the bus that people rushed over. "My girlfriend's been shot," I told them, "I was just calling her."

The sudden loss of her life, such a vibrant candidate to a midnight murder, made me stop and remind myself to live each day stress free and to try, if possible, to be kind. What had she done to be killed? It was a HIT! What did she know, or do? I couldn't imagine why anyone had killed Ronni!

Blow number two occurred only a few weeks later during Christmas week. I was with my darling friend Maria Floyd, the wife of the champion golfer Raymond Floyd, whose Palm Beach home I stayed in when I appeared in the Neiman Marcus store there. I always stayed with Maria. I stayed with her every year for 30 years. Her home was a dream, her life with handsome Raymond was a dream, and her home at Christmas time was the dream of dreams. The house was always magnificently decorated for the holidays, from top to bottom, and both Maria and Raymond loved to cook southern-style for their guests. Their home was an American palace. Photos of Raymond with all the American Presidents lined the walls of their red velvet bar.

Maria and I had spent the day on the beach with her family the previous year and I keep this happy photo of us next to my bed because the next day, out of nowhere, Maria found out she was bleeding internally and was told she had cancer with only months to live. Before that, she had never been sick. She was exactly my age, sixty-six. She was brave and she died the next summer.

What to do? What should I do? My life had changed because of these tragedies of two of my girlfriends.

I went home to my farm, to my husband, to my dogs, and to my ninety-year-old parents who had moved in to live with us, and I saw everyone and everything differently. I had lived my fashion life; I had been making and selling dresses since I

My day at the beach with Maria Floyd

was twelve. Now, I just wanted to stay home, feed my chickens, smell my roses, and write and write about my crazy life.

My life was a life that nobody believed. I had learned lessons from some of the world's most extraordinary women. When I had "girlfriends talk," when I told stories of my experiences with these women, jaws would drop. I would write and write about what I had learned from my world-famous, powerful mentors and pass these lessons on to others.

*My first bridal sketch
in 1957 at age 14.*

"You have to learn the rules of the game. And then you have to play better than anyone else."

ALBERT EINSTEIN

Learning the Rules of the Game: My First Loves

learned much about life and relationships while young and in love, and I want to share that wisdom with you.

My Idol

As a teenager in Chevy Chase, my bedroom walls were plastered with photos of men I would meet, and sometimes seduce, later in life: Elvis, Marlon, Paul, and Warren. But my ultimate heartthrob was the great sports hero of my time, Mickey Mantle. Blond hair, blue eyes, switch hitter for the champion baseball team the New York Yankees. Marilyn Monroe had Joe DiMaggio, but I "had" Mickey Mantle.

Ever since I was eight years old, I went to every Yankees game that came to Washington and I was finally invited to sit next to the Yankee dugout. At twelve, but looking eighteen, wearing a tight, belted, cashmere sweater and a Vicky-design sheath skirt with a high back slit, I was definitely jail bait.

Mickey never got me into bed, of course, we just fan-flirted, but he was hooked by my baseball expertise. "Hit one for me,"

I would yell when the Yankees needed a home run. I screamed at him when he struck out. I helped him through slumps and sometimes followed him to New York, (with my grandfather) to Yankee Stadium, to push up his home run records. After every game I attended he gave me his batters line-up card that he signed "To Vickey love Mickey," so he changed how I spelled my name. Now my labels read Vicky Tiel, not Vickie Tiel, thanks to my darling Mickey.

Catching the All American

Tom Bacas, at eleven years old, was my first *realistic* love after Magic Mickey. Tom was the most handsome boy in our elementary school. He was a Greek Orthodox, straight-A student, class President, and captain of the football team, but Tom "hated" girls. My sixth-grade love was the ultimate challenge, my complete opposite, and my female classmates, my "girlfriends," were ready for me to conquer him. I did everything without doing anything, no phone calls, no passed notes! I just practiced my seductive walks, looks, stares, and smiles, but sadly I got nothing from Tom. We were friends and nothing more. Then I moved to Maryland and Tom stayed in downtown Washington. Yet, never one to give up, even after six years, I was at last Tom's date to his senior prom at Anacostia High, before he took off to Harvard. On prom night, at the overnight party on the Ocean City beach, we came close to having sex. We did have an affair later, when he was at Harvard, and I got to spend the night at Eliot House. My patience and persistence proved that everything is possible if you are determined. Sadly, Tom was not the man for wild and crazy me.

Jimmy Rowe—My Twin

At Kensington Junior High, my sweet-heart was Jimmy Rowe, who is still a pal today. Blue-eyed, blond, and gorgeous, I had a fashion trick that allowed me to make sure it was "hands off" for my female classmates. I had us dressed in matching styles and colors every day for seventh and eighth grades. We would phone each other before school and organize our matching outfits. We really looked adorable at school dances, as we blended into one on the dance floor. To stake your claim and brand your man, coordinate your colors in more ways than one!

The Already Taken Man

At Bethesda–Chevy Chase High School, it was rough. All the good men were already taken. Just as in real life where there are so few good and totally available men walking around. Yet, a woman must not give up when an UNMARRIED man is already taken. (I do not believe in "taking" a married man. My first husband was married when we met and he lied about it, saying he was getting a divorce. This was tragic for his family. He was a cheater. He cheated on me and wives number one and two before me, and wives four and five after me.)

How do you get your single man away from another sweetheart? He cannot ask you out on a date, that would be cheating. Instead, get him to meet you someplace that is not a date. Try the grocery store, the library, an art exhibit, some-place neutral. Michael, my first high school crush, avoided his steady one Sunday and asked to meet me at his Church. I was not his religion but I would have joined the Foreign Legion. I tried out my Sixty-Second Seduction Method on him and it worked. (You stare at him, look at your best feature, my breasts, and back at his eyes, then smile.)

Michael Wilbourn was a grade ahead and the high school's moody actor. We met while he performed "The Glass Menagerie" and played the Gentleman Caller, a role my parents were to know only too well. He was tall, blue-eyed, sensitive, and very poetic wearing his turtlenecks and baggy corduroy pants, our very own James Dean. The girls were all in love with him. He had been going steady with a girl in his class for a year but we fell in love and they broke up. We had a long romance, several years, and broke up when I moved to Paris at nineteen and started dating Woody Allen and a gorgeous German boy with a motorcycle.

A Gentle First Lover

A gentle first lover is a prerequisite. Mothers need to teach this to their daughters. The best first lovers are young men, young boyfriends who are groomed in tenderness, friendship, and sweet passion. A gentle touch makes fear go away.

Neurotic sex is often repetitive of early disasters. Pain in sex can be exciting later in life, but not at first. Early lessons in love give us practice for knowing what we want and getting healthy responses.

Not everyone is equally sexual. You can love someone totally opposite in every aspect, except sex. I believe we are sexual on a scale from one to ten, and we must partner with our same sexual number. In sex, we need to find our match for there to be fire and sparks. When your bodies touch, sex vibrates, yin and yang, back and forth. Once the charge goes away for too long, it does not come back. This is the doomsday for a marriage.

Men Who See Women as Objects

As long as women are seen as objects to be bought and tossed, women must do whatever they can to get a "good man." However, today more and more women in Western countries are rejecting this ancient behavior and these women are the ones finding the men that they want and they love. The Middle Eastern world is soon catching up, and, within a generation, women there will reject the men that want to shame them and "buy" them. Shame is a bullying tactic to keep women in their place and a NO SHAME policy is only a matter of time for the Eastern woman.

Kimball Highlights from our School Paper

Habits
Habits are important,
For you and me.
They bring better manners,
As you'll plainly see.
1   brush your teeth
    Regularly,
    For health and attractiveness,
    It's easy as you'll see.
2   is your posture,
    Now you must stand up straight
    For you'll look better,
    And really really feel great.
3   is rest,
    You need plenty of that,
    So when you play,
    You can really swing the bat.
4   is your fingernails,
    The girls should keep them clean,
    And don't ever bite them,
    So they'll really look keen.
5   is the way you dress,
    Yes you should keep nice and neat,
    Then you'll really be,
    A pretty sight from head to feet.

Vickie Tiel, Grade 6, April 4, 1955

Quotes in The Pinetree *yearbook, 1961. My friends already knew I was going to partner with Elizabeth Taylor.*

"I was street smart,
but unfortunately the street
was Rodeo Drive."

CARRIE FISHER

Confidence: First Lessons in Seduction

Still waters run deep, especially on the banks of the Potomac River in Washington D.C., the most sexually-frustrated, uptight town in the United States, that produced the most sexually avant-garde children of the '60s: Warren Beatty, Shirley MacLaine, Goldie Hawn, Jim Morrison, and myself! Wallis Simpson, the Duchess of Windsor, whose fling broke up the English throne, was from nearby Baltimore.

In the south, the reigning heroine of the twentieth century was Scarlett O'Hara, a relentless powerhouse who closed the most famous film in the world, *Gone with the Wind,* with some powerful words. Scarlett's words became my mantra: "I'll Think About it Tomorrow."

I WILL NOT GET UPSET TODAY, I WILL FIGURE IT OUT TOMORROW WITH MORE INFORMATION.

I was born boy crazy. I wanted to spend all my time with boys in tree houses. I was an only child and had no brother, yet boys did not intimidate me. On the contrary, their friendship and admiration boosted my self-esteem. I knew what it was to be a '50s female, cooking and cleaning, but it was my hanging out in the trees with boys and watching long baseball games that would open my eyes to understanding the male and give me the confidence to be around boys and later men.

In the "Father's Knows Best" world of the 50s, wives wore aprons and daughters obeyed. Somehow, I grew up wanting to be equal to men and I realized that I would need to change my little Maryland world. My parents controlled what I bought with their money, so, at twelve years old, I decided to make my own money by sewing and selling clothes. I bought my own telephone line for my bedroom, put my name in the phone book, and began Vicky Tiel Fashion.

As I grew into a teenager, I realized that other young girls did not have my skills with males. They would come to me for advice on how to behave with boys. Thus, my future career began. I was motivated at an early age to become an expert on how to help other females attract men and I would teach girls about how to please men while *always* pleasing themselves. I was a born saleswoman and when I sold dresses, I sold CONFIDENCE.

Growing up, Chevy Chase, Maryland was one of the wealthiest and definitely the most conservative community in Conservative Washington. Almost everyone worked for the government, nobody could rock the boat. Yet, Washington D.C. was where the good girls ironed their cotton bras into points and were waiting to become '60s rebels.

These were the Eisenhower years. The teenage dream boy was Ricky Nelson. At twelve, I met him at a rock concert and he invited me backstage. Why did Ricky pick me out of the front row? I was visibly impossible to overlook, looking like I was eighteen with my Pucci print, skin-tight, fitted dress, pointed

breasts, and an Elizabeth Taylor haircut. I had worn my first design that I sewed myself to the concert and it worked. I had been noticed by a star! A fashion career was born.

I went to a New York fashion college, Parsons School of Design. By night, I sewed my way into a shop in my apartment, dressing hot, young, Greenwich Village men in leather pants and women in New York's first leather miniskirt. My fashion business paid for my move to Paris after graduation.

In dressing women there, while only twenty, I discovered that there are three types of women: the Sexpot (Marilyn Monroe), the Farmer's Wife or Clever Girl-Next-Door (Debbie Reynolds), and the Cool, Intellectual Woman (Grace Kelly). In today's world, they would be Mariah Carey, Jennifer Lawrence, and Meryl Streep. My ideal woman was all three in one. Sexy, strong, and classy. My desire was to combine all three and become powerful. I would be brainy, cool, and determined. Most of all, DETERMINED to never give up. My role models growing up as a child were Elizabeth Taylor and Natalie Wood, both of whom I amazingly got to dress later in life and both became my girlfriends. Only after I knew them did I realize that their protective Hollywood childhood did not allow them to "experience men as little boys," and they did not know as much about men as I did.

Having seduced the hottest man in Greenwich Village with an outfit alone was proof of what I learned at twelve, when I made my first sale of a felt circle skirt to my potluck friend. A skirt that I sewed in Kensington Junior High School Home Economics Class taught me the best lesson of my life, that creating fashion was how I could become powerful, earning my own money and influencing women to become hot and powerful too! Goodbye to "Mother Knows Best," with her pointed bras and aprons. Look out Paris, here I come.

Barbra StreisAND

blue leather jumpsuit 1973 shopping at Bendel's with her dog

Vicky Tiel

"Take care of all your memories,
for you cannot relive them."

BOB DYLAN

Peaches LaTour on Jones Street

I left for college in the Fall of 1961 and moved to Greenwich Village in New York, where my first home ever was a floor-through pink brownstone on Jones Street. My first job was passing the hat for my boyfriend, Steve DeNaut, a gorgeous folksinger at the Café Wha? I also passed the hat for Bobby Zimmerman (later called Bob Dylan).

Steve named me "Peaches LaTour," a name that stuck. When I landed my first job in Paris, making the costumes for the film *What's New Pussycat?*, the writer of the film, Woody Allen, saw me in the halls of Billancourt Studios and yelled out for all the world to hear, "What are you doing in Paris, Peaches LaTour?"

I replied, "I'm doing your film."

Peaches La Tour

Vicky Tiel
1962
items sold
in the
Village

"Forget about the fast lane. If you really want to fly, harness your power to your passion."

OPRAH WINFREY

What is Feminine Power?

Feminine Power is the freedom to make your own decisions, to think and speak your own thoughts, to spend time with whomever you choose, and to follow your dreams on how to live your life.

Feminine Power is the art of letting go of power, as taught by Sun Tzu in "The Art of War," by using quiet power and not "dancing" with an aggressor, until they are encircled and quietly defeated. Appearing not powerful is a strategy that is very hard for males and easy for females, and thus gives females a huge advantage.

Yet, Feminine Power is not defined by other people's definition, or society's definition, of feminine power: it is "What I should be and what I do."

Women are by nature peaceful and nurturing. It seems almost all the bloodshed on earth is caused by men.

Women choose love over power; therefore, women are more powerful. Women throughout the ages embrace the spiritual, extend kindness and forgiveness, and teach these concepts to children.

Absolute power and the art of letting go is INVISIBLE, FEMININE, AND PURE, LOVING ENERGY.

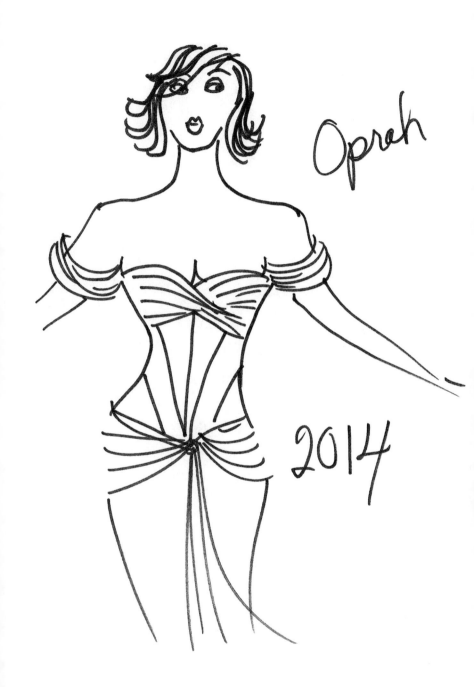

Love life, live for love, love yourself,
love everyone and everything
around you, let go of anger,
and forgive and you will become
The Absolute Woman.

VICKY TIEL

Ten Points to Achieve Feminine Power

1. **Follow Your Dreams**
   Even though you are told you can't do something because you are a woman, don't believe anybody. Do what you love and what you do easily. (I was told I wasn't good enough to design on Seventh Ave, but I went to Paris and succeeded.) Choose what you love and who you love.

2. **Don't Dance with Crazies**
   Ignore everyone who is mean or cruel to you, including family. When you ignore people, they leave you alone. When you leave a bear or a snake alone, they sense it and walk away. On my wilderness farm, I always tell wild animals in a soft voice "You're Beautiful" and they sense your love and drop attack mode.

3. **Conceit is Self-Given, Be Careful**
   Don't live a "me-me" life. Live to help other people and help animals and all life.

4. **No Sex for Shoes**

   Make your own money and buy your own shoes. You don't need men for money and YOU CHOOSE WHO YOU HAVE SEX WITH.

5. **You Are What You Drink**

   We are eighty percent liquid, so diet and health should start with your drink.

6. **When You Wash the Dishes, Wash the Dishes**

   From the teachings of Ram Dass, "Be Here Now" and live in the moment. "Dead yesterday and unborn tomorrow, why worry if today be sweet."

7. **Marry the Man Who Really Loves You**

   Don't chase after a man, ever! Men are everywhere. Go for the one who really loves you.

8. **Be Yourself, Everyone Else Is Already Taken**

   Be happy with who you are. Don't be concerned with how you are perceived by others. If you love soft dresses, wear them. Dress how you yourself like to be perceived. Work on the jobs that make you happy, no matter if it's repairing cars or flying airplanes or teaching.

9. **Live for Love, Love Every Second of Your Life, God Is Love**

   Always look for positive things that happen, don't hold on to the negative things and brush them off. Be happy that you are alive.

10. **For Personal Peace, Become One with Nature**

Try to meditate, find a calm time to sit, look, and love the earth and all its beauty. Find beauty everywhere you go. Smile! Smiling and happiness adds at least ten years to your life.

Martha
Stewart

1985

black lace
black jersey
skirt

Martha's
first top cover

Vicky Tiel

What Is Not Feminine Power?

1. Having someone pay for you other than a bank; needing to ask someone for money to buy shoes, a computer, a house.

2. Having someone dictate how you spend your time.

3. Having someone tell you what to think.

4. Having sex with someone you do not desire.

5. Holding anger in your heart.

6. Being denied an education because you are a woman.

7. Acting like a bossy man.

Princess Stephanie of Monaco 1984

Bubble dress in fushia toffetta Matching gloves and bag

worn at Bal de Croix Rouge

Vicky Tiel

"All women are goddesses and it's just a matter of letting that goddess power shine and if you don't try to be the biggest and baddest damn goddess you can be, you are selling yourself short!"

KIMORA LEE SIMMONS

The Return of Goddess Power Is Inevitable

Women ruled Planet Earth for 35,000 years, and very few women today know this fact. It was called **Goddess Power**, as women were Goddess-mothers of Mother Earth.

Men have only ruled Earth for about 4000 years, since monotheistic religion made women give up their power to form families and try and keep men monogamous.

But that can change once women gain complete equality on Planet Earth.

Women changing their behavior once they understand Goddess Power is inevitable. It will come, the only question is WHEN.

As I walked down the street in Manhattan, I saw a tall, beautiful, young girl wearing a black T-shirt with large white letters that read: Young Powerful Woman.

"A woman is like a tea bag,
you can't tell how strong she is
until you put her in hot water."

ELEANOR ROOSEVELT

Feminine Power, My Way

In the 1970s, I was in San Francisco on TV before an I. Magnin Couture fashion appearance. Their publicity department had arranged for an early morning local TV show with three famous feminist authors and myself. The one I had heard of was Betty Friedan, who wrote "The Feminine Mystique," the book that started it all. I was the only woman at that long table that was dressed like a fancy French woman. All the others were dressed in crisp, white men shirts or tweed jackets, and I was in a colorful wrap dress with a low-cut décolletage, covered in ropes of beads, and big diamond rings on my fingers.

The other famous ladies gave me the Bully Look, as I spoke about working women. Then, one of them put me down on air, mostly about my ultra-feminine attire, saying that I was dressed only to attract men. I couldn't hold myself back and I replied, "Yes, I like men, and I'm the *only* one here who has owned a company in a foreign country since the age of twenty, the only one who employs twenty-five women, while you all write books in bed."

Dressing the models for my first Vicky Tiel Paris fashion show at Hotel Intercontinental, 1971.

"I love to farm and shoot guys and wreck cars."

LEE-GRACE DOUGHERTY

About Security or "Don't Dance with Crazies"

My friend Sue Bloomberg tells me I'm the most secure person she has ever met, except for her ex, Michael, who was the brilliant mayor of New York. How did I become the confident cheerleader turned Parisian/American fashion designer that advises the world's richest women on how to behave? How did this happen? Maybe, as Lady Gaga says, I was "born that way," but I want to share my history, so that maybe it will help others.

As a young girl, I did not hang out in groups of girls, I did not join clubs or girl cliques, I did not try to be popular. I only hung out with the cutest boys in the school. I guess I was considered wild. One girlfriend, Amy, was forbidden to "play" with me, simply because I was always surrounded by boys. She was not allowed to date, even in eleventh grade, so we would meet at the local drugstore and have two sixteen-year-olds pick us up in their cars.

There are always mean people who say mean things. I ignored them and just smiled at any nasty comments. I hung out with sweet people, fun people, artsy people. I felt sorry for the bullies and pitied them, as I thought they were most likely jealous or crazy. By ignoring bullies, they ignored me and they picked on others who were more easily hurt by them.

I had excuses. I could have been a mess. I was an only child and the only "divorced child" in my school in 1950. I had a moody Mom, an artist who spent all her time painting, but I had a wonderful Grandma who watched over me. I did not have negative thoughts about Mom, but instead positive thoughts about Grandma, who was a better cook. I turned everything into wonderful, blessed, beautiful. Ugly and evil did not enter my thoughts; as a childhood artist myself, all I wanted was to see beauty everywhere.

At Kensington Junior High, I became a cheerleader when I was twelve years old, and for five years (except for learning to speak French) I didn't learn about much in school besides football, basketball, soccer, and golf. I mostly learned about boys and what they loved, because I rode weekly to the opposing games on buses with the darling sports-star athletes.

Oh yes...and I did learn to sew.

Earning my own money to have my own private life became necessary at twelve years old, when I was told that I couldn't have my own telephone in my room for private conversations with my new sporty boyfriends. In the "pre-cellphone world," our mothers could overhear everything and even my mother could bully me.

The solution was, quite simply, TO MAKE MY OWN MONEY AND BUY MY OWN PHONE AND NOT ASK ANYBODY FOR ANYTHING. HAVING MY OWN MONEY GAVE ME POWER TO IGNORE ANY NASTY OR NEGA-TIVE COMMENTS.

I NEEDED TO BE COMPLETELY INDEPENDENT. YES! FREE TO BE ME! I EVEN HAD MY NAME, VICKY TIEL, PUT IN THE CHEVY CHASE, MARYLAND PHONE BOOK.

Making clothes for my rich girlfriends was my solution, and though I didn't learn much in school, I did learn one magical thing that made my entire life, I LEARNED TO SELL. "YOU HAVE TO HAVE THIS" became my mantra. I started with circle skirts and caftans and sold them to my classmates for twenty-five dollars in the '50s, and I never had to ask for money for the special fashion needs of a teenager. I saved and bought a mink-lined, hooded, cream cashmere coat at sixteen years old! I also bought the most expensive silk nightgown and matching robe ever for sale in Garfinkel's, Washington D.C.'s poshest store. It cost 140 dollars in 1959; I was sixteen and wore it in front of my bedroom mirror. Later, I wore it in Paris when I was with Hollywood Ron, my first husband, Elvis Presley's make up man, five years later.

I knew it would come in handy.

WE ARE ALL GOOD AT SOMETHING, SO LEARN YOUNG WHAT YOUR TALENT IS AND NEVER LET GO. Make that money and train your children to do the same. After the age of twelve, teach your children to perform a job. Pay them minimum wage to mow the lawn, take out the trash, paint the walls, or do the dishes. Having their own bank account and income is a great way to begin a PROFITABLE working life. As they get older, teach your children to work at a job they love.

In my fashion career, I have been treated horribly by many other designers over my long tenure. Once in Bergdorf, another designer, on the opposite side of the fourth floor, would not appear in the store if I came in, even just to fit a client in my dressing room. I had to be snuck in. I did not complain to management—I let the other designer live in her anger.

At a fancy ball in New York, the most famous American female designer put me down in front of several celebrities. I was wearing a mini and I just smiled at her and I did not reply; I just stared at her horrible, fat knees and looked up at her eyes.

Security leads to being powerful. How do you become a completely secure woman? Learn about boys and what they like, as they are half the planet. Learn to be best friends with men as their equals, just like you are best friends with women. Have no fear of men. You will have no fear of men if you love and understand them. Find lady friends who are up tempo and not depressed. Find girlfriends who are soul-mates and be there for them and help them throughout their life. Always give. They will be there for you to give advice when you need it.

Find what you love to do, while you are young, as practice makes perfect. I loved drawing and sewing. I loved looking wonderful. So, I became an artist and a dress designer.

Look in the mirror at your best friend and love her, really love her. If you do that, you don't have to think about yourself all the time.

Find a mentor when you are young. Become a mentor when you are old.

Ignore negative sentences, turn all the evil words you hear from family, friends, the workplace, even strangers; turn the evil words from the "crazies" into something totally opposite, smile at the crazies and walk away.

DO NOT DANCE WITH CRAZIES...put that on a T-shirt, write it on your fridge.

"You stupid bitch" becomes "You are the cleverest girl on the planet."

Just Smile. No one can hurt you.

Ewa Aulin
in "Candy"
1967

Scene with
Marlon Brando
who plays the Guru

White jersey wrap
around dress
square
ties behind
Neck

VickyTiel

"*Everything you see I owe to spaghetti.*"

SOPHIA LOREN

You Are How You Are Perceived?

When I went to Parsons School of Design in January 1962, I was placed at a table of twenty girls and two boys who all wanted to be fashion designers. The girl next to me, at the end of the table, was Mary Alice Orito and the girl opposite me was my future design partner, Mia Fonssagrives. You could not have found three more different, young, female fashion students.

Mary Alice was from Bonner Springs, Kansas, where she lived above her mother's electrical hardware store. Mia grew up across the street from the Manhattan Bloomingdale's on 61st and Third and had a weekend farm on Huntington, Long Island. Her stepfather was *Vogue* photographer Irving Penn and her mother wasSwedish model Lisa Fonssagrives. I grew up in the posh suburbs of Washington D.C. where I was a cheerleader at Bethesda–Chevy Chase and my grandfather was a spy.

After I gave up my Manhattan office in 2011 and my apartment sold, I would stay with my former classmate, Mary Alice, whenever I came to New York. She had been a costume designer for the TV show, *Search for Tomorrow*, for twenty years, but when all the TV shows went on strike in 1988, she left fashion to become a talk therapist and life coach. (She also returned to work as an artist and became President of National Association of Women's Artists.)

I asked Mary Alice over our breakfast of Belgian waffles at Petite Abeille, our favorite French cafe in downtown Manhattan, "What is the main reason people visit you? Why do they see a shrink? What is their main concern, their main illness?" I was expecting to hear that it was their love life, or their drug addiction, or their kids, but no, she said, much to my surprise, "THE MAIN ISSUE WITH MY PATIENTS IS THEIR CONCERN OF HOW THEY ARE PERCEIVED!"

WHAT? I was in shock. Who cared about that? Well, apparently, everybody but me. I never even think about how I'm perceived, which is probably why I was successful my fifty-year fashion career, as I never wondered for a second about this.

I know women, even most young designers, would never walk down the street looking like I did in 1963 with thigh-high skirts and see-thru lace tops. I paid no attention to the shocked looks of others; I just wanted my picture taken to help me sell product. I did not concern myself and worry about how I looked, I wanted to inspire others to wear my designs, to SELL.

Why is how others see us the most important problem of human beings? Why are we born so unconfident? Fear, lack of courage, insecurity? What do we need to do to ourselves to become powerful?

Now I understood why I'd always given advice to my clients while I was selling them my dresses. They lacked my confidence. They were normal; I was not normal. I was born this odd way. I was given a gift from the higher powers that be, to not "give a damn" what anyone thought of me, just to be true to myself.

I was lucky to have my mother, Ethel Kipnes, a truly amazing artist who pretty much left me alone so she could paint every day, and a grandmother, Fanny Kipnes, who looked after me and encouraged me, always telling me that I was perfect. My father, David Tiel, made me work for my money, and my stepfather, Milton Meisels, came to Paris when I opened my shop and gave me a piece of paper with a line down the center, the words "IN" and "OUT" separated. He said the IN is your money you make each week and the OUT is the money you spend. Make sure the IN side has more money than the OUT side. Make this chart every month. They all helped me to get where I am.

Mary Alice told me, "The higher power, or karma, places people in our path to point us in the 'right' direction. We never do it alone, sometimes we have more awareness than other times, and sometimes we pick the right path, but we have to find it, we have to see the breadcrumbs laid there by others."

My advice to my dress clients that I learned over fifty years is this: love yourself, love every second of your life, be happy no matter what happens, it's God's will, and DO NOT DANCE with anyone negative, just smile at them and stay happy. If people make you unhappy, just avoid them, but if you can't, just smile and send them loving energy. Don't worry, eventually they give up their negative game and find others to DANCE with.

The only thing that matters in life is to love yourself and be happy, and this way you will stop any negative thinking, forgive anything negative, and learn to let go and love others. And of course, for women I advise ALWAYS MAKE YOUR OWN MONEY AND WORK FOREVER. THEN YOU REALLY CAN LOVE YOURSELF AS YOU ARE THE TRUE BOSS OF YOU.

"Saturday Night Fever" 1977

white jersey dress gold belt slit sleeves slit skirt

dance scene where she meets John Travolta

Vicky Tiel

"I'm not afraid of death because
I don't believe in it. It's just getting
out of one car, and into another."

JOHN LENNON

Three Powerful Women and the Highway to Happiness

Helena Rubinstein, Elizabeth Arden, and Coco Chanel were the first three successful, self-made women of the twentieth century, and funny enough they were all in the business of fashion and beauty.

Helena Rubinstein, born in 1872, was a penniless, Jewish-Polish immigrant when she arrived in Australia. She opened her first beauty salon before World War I in Melbourne with her own face cream.

Tiny, at only 4' 10", Helena built a multi-million-dollar empire from the world's first cream with lanolin (an ingredient she discovered in Australia). She opened beauty salons in Paris and later in New York, where she never had a loan from a bank, or a generous husband, as Helena made and managed all her own money, and wisely invested in one of the world's greatest art collections. She threw the most elaborate parties in Paris, on her rooftop overlooking the Seine. She socialized with high society, French royalty, and Europe's great artists and musicians. Helena married her third husband, a Duke, who was twenty-three years younger.

As a student, I was shown her Paris apartment on the Île Saint-Louis and dreamt of living nearby. Twenty years later, I found my dream home just meters down the river with the same view.

Elizabeth Arden, born in 1878, in Ontario, Canada, had a dream to open beauty salons. She went to Paris to learn skin care, opened 150 salons in America, and created over 1000 products, and never had a backer. She taught all the women of the world to cover their entire face with makeup and to wear lipstick, something previously done only by prostitutes and lower-class women. She was awarded the French Legion D'Honor, and that's rare for a Canadian, let alone a woman.

Gabrielle "Coco" Chanel was born in 1883 in the south of France to a single mother so poor they only had a dirt floor. Coco was so ambitious as a teenager that she began to create and sell hats in her provincial village. Hats became clothes. Coco invented jersey, sportswear, ladies in pants, and the little black dress. She basically invented what ladies wear on Planet Earth.

In 1925 she created her first fragrance, Chanel No 5. When she was the first to license her fragrance to Bourjois (owned by Pierre Wertheimer) in 1947, she received one million a year, quite a lot after the war, and she also asked Wertheimer to pay all her living expenses. He did.

She also was the first designer to license her name.

Coco was my heroine when I was a student, and she became my mentor, as I met her just before her death on a special night at a dinner party arranged by Elizabeth Taylor, when Coco held my hands and advised me to make a perfume. I don't make twenty-five million a year, but I have a nice lifestyle thanks to Coco. She worked until the end. On her last night, she sold a dress and went from her shop on the Rue Cambon to her home at the Ritz Hotel where she died.

Helena Rubinstein lived until ninety-two. Elizabeth Arden and Coco Chanel lived to be eighty-seven.

These three women lived twenty years longer than women were expected to live in the 1970s. All three women worked nonstop until they died.

These three women showed that a life of financial independence, of women making their own money from selling their own products that they personally created and never needing loans, was a highway to happiness that I was wise enough to copy.

1968
Brigitte
Bardot

wears a polka
dot yellow string
bikini

in St. Tropez

terry cloth stretch
jersey
with cord
string ties

VickyTiel

"Civilization begins with a rose."
(A Rose is a Clitoris.)

GERTRUDE STEIN

Sexual Revolution of the '60s

The Sexual Revolution started in the late '50s in Paris with two movies and two big movie stars: Brigitte Bardot in *...And God Created Woman* in 1956 and Jean-Paul Belmondo in *Breathless* in 1960.

Brigitte had real sex (to completion) on set, on camera, with her co-star who later became her permanent lover, Jean-Louis Trintignant, while her desolate husband, the film's director, Roger Vadim, directed the scene. Her marriage was over at that moment, but free love was born. The Queen of the Sexual Revolution was Brigitte, and women everywhere worldwide copied her hair, her makeup, and the first, tiny, polka-dot bikini she barely wore at the Cannes Film Festival of 1956 along with her full skirt, pink gingham, low cut, lace-trimmed dress. Both styles went global as Brigitte launched the cinematic female empowerment revolution.

Jean-Paul Belmondo had casual sex all over the movie *Breathless* with an American, Jean Seberg, and at last America's puritanical image was fini! The film brought New Wave

Cinema to the forefront in 1961, with Jean-Luc Godard, the brilliant director who changed how movies were shot as well. Of course, it was France that changed sexual behavior on the planet. Jean Seberg, at the end of the film, copies Belmondo's smile and gesture as she fingers her lips in a close up, "I GOT HIM GOOD." The women of the '60s followed these two women and freed themselves to make their own money and sleep with whomever they desired. The good virgin bride, the handpicked woman, the old-time image of marriage became antiquated in the Western World. Women now had a choice of any man they wanted. As Brigitte Bardot toyed with the gorgeous men in ...*And God Created Woman*, including her desolate husband, the director, she showed the world that she chose the man. She showed that "GOD CREATED WOMEN WHO COULD CHOOSE."

Earlier on in American Cinema, Jane Russell showed her big breasts in *Outlaw* and Marilyn Monroe brought naive extreme sexuality to the screen, in *Some Like It Hot*, but it was the French New Wave Cinema that brought empowered, modern, sexual women to the screen; women with their own money, women choosing their own men on their terms, and women dumping their men as they pleased.

Women are not the only animal that choose their males, but women are such powerful animals that the human males cannot have sex from behind, as all animals must do. The human female is the only animal (except bonobos, whales, and dolphins) that makes her male face her for sex.

Fashion has a lot to do with the Sexual Revolution of the '60s. Women could choose their style and express themselves. Women were no longer forced by society, or their husbands, to wear a certain look. Women after the '60s could choose how they wanted to be perceived and could change their style as they saw fit, going from long, pleated, Gypsy skirts and ruffled tops, to thigh-high boots and minis the next day. Fashion, mass fashion, became a worldwide money-making business.

Women choosing their men was not a new thing on Planet Earth. From 35000 to 2500 BC when Goddess Culture ruled, women used men to hunt and build shelter and farm. Men were replaceable.

Dressing in a hot, sexual style did not mean the woman wearing it was a stripper or a hooker, it meant that she was expressing herself and was now *at last* free to do so.

I dressed in minis and see-thru tops in the '60s while owning my own company, Mia-Vicky, and making hundreds of thousands of dollars a year. While wearing only what I desired to wear each day, I never had a man attack me on the streets, only stare, and the few who attacked me in private, never succeeded.

Will the #MeToo movement of today change Middle East fashion? I used to sell my sexy gowns to five shops in Beirut in the early '70s and dressed many Iranian women until 1979. That year the wealthy escaped and many moved to Paris. (Perhaps to be near their couturiers?) Will the young Muslim women one day join the fashions of the rest of the world? We will see.

Jean Seberg 1971

Vicky Tiel

Publicist Yanou Collart, Jean-Paul Belmondo, and Vicky lunch at the Brasserie Lipp.

"I did not just fall in love.
I made a parachute jump."

ZORA NEALE HURSTON

Find a Man that Puts You First

My advice on "finding a man" comes from what I learned from the thousands of women I personally dressed. When they are naked in the dressing room, women tell me everything! Women choose men, men do not choose women. Half the people walking on the planet are men, so for a woman to say 'there's nobody for me' means that she is not really looking. We grow up with fantasies of movie stars and rock stars, athletes and legends, and even power brokers, but my advice is this:

Take the first man who comes along who really wants YOU! Who really loves YOU. Why waste time on a man who you must pursue? Choose the one who loves you, makes love to you, and has most of the qualities you desire. Nobody has all the qualities you desire; nobody gets the whole pie. But, pick a man who *thinks* you are the whole pie.

Life has a funny way of putting Mr. Right in front of you. It's our job as women to recognize him.

Wanting the man who wants YOU is a problem. He's too short, he didn't go to MIT, he can't speak French, he's a Geek (not a Greek), I've heard it all, but really! Why waste a second on a man not madly in love with you? Find a man who wants you to be his life partner, and who wants to satisfy you in bed for hours before he satisfies himself.

This man will inspire you to grow, as he thinks you're the greatest. Thus, you will become the greatest.

Wanting a man who inspires you to grow, who thinks you're the greatest, is better than any college degree, as he will inspire you to get degrees, open companies, and learn to parachute from planes, and then when you retire and move to the mountains you will buy a cabin and write a book. You will follow your dreams as his love and passion will inspire you.

When I wanted to take all my life savings twenty-five years ago and invest in a perfume business, my younger fisherman husband said KNOCK YOURSELF OUT. My father, my previous businessman fiancée, my "party animal" first husband, all would have forbidden me to risk everything I saved for following my dream.

Learn to love the person, not the exterior. Learn to love them because they truly love you. Of course, the outside must be pleasing, but perfect does not exist. I've met perfect men, but there is always something. Generally perfect movie stars are in love with themselves and their agents and you get ten minutes with them.

The young female of today, when questioned about their choice of a mate, goes immediately to their outward appearance, clothes, hairstyle, weight, height, their choice of car... as the millennials are more superficial and they admit it. However, by the time the second or third bad boyfriend comes into their bed, they generally open their eyes and a "good man" wins their heart.

Strong women don't need a competitor as a partner, whose jealousy will knock her down. My first husband was an artist with ups and downs, and my constant success unnerved him. An artist needs an agent or an accountant as a husband, not a competitive artist.

A strong woman doesn't need a competitor but a partner who can do what she can't or won't. Strong women don't need a man for money; a strong woman should make her own money and find a partner who completes her.

Amen.

Goldie Hawn

1983

"13 B"
peach satin
duchesse
wrap
dress
with big
bow

Vicky Tiel

"Knowing others is wisdom..."

LAO TZU

Ten Tips for Recognizing the Right Man

1. It is impossible to say "There is nobody for me." IMPOS-SIBLE! Women who say that are not really looking, as they don't want to admit that they don't want a man or simply they just don't want any more sex. These women could be a one or two or a three (on the lower end of the scale from one to ten in sexuality).
2. Men are everywhere. There is someone for everyone, at every age. Choose don't chase.
3. Look your best (you should dress your best at all times anyway). But if you are not at your best, work on your beauty, fashion, and diet, and pull yourself up and out, and go where men are without women. Start your make-over in a hip beauty salon and LISTEN.
4. Change your routine. Join healthy exercise groups. Go to sports events with friends. Join dating sites, if you can't meet a man in person (because men lie online). Do not go into any strange man's home please! Do meet a new man at a chic cafe, or a restaurant, BUT NOT EVER

at a bar, as that is a likely place for an alcoholic. If you are an alcoholic, go to an AA or NA meeting, and get a clean man there who is single and a sponsor with many years sober. If a first date has more than two drinks, beware.

5. Be on time. Try to have a first date anywhere but a bar. Try a sports event, a walk, a gym, a sports game, golf, or bowling.

6. Take your time. Does your conversation flow?

7. Does he initiate a second date quickly? Someone who doesn't ask to see you again is not interested. Remember, choose the man who is crazy about you. Do you need a second date to be sure? Sometimes first dates have been disastrous and yet couples continue and laugh about them on their weddings.

8. Is he who he says he is? This takes time to find out. So many people lie.

9. Offer to split the check. This shows you are your own person.

10. Is he reliable, respectful, and kind to animals?

Woman's Guide to Love and Lasting Relationships

* Find a man who makes you laugh
* Find a man who has a good job and can cook
* Find a man who is honest
* Find a man who is awesome in bed
* Most of all, it is very important that these five men don't meet.

"Yoko Ono"
1994

Black draped
jersey
and black jet
beadeds

Yoko recieves John, Lennon's
award introduction
to Rock + Roll Hall of
Fame -
re-unites with Paul McCartney

Vicky Tiel

"One day I will find Mr. Right...
and he will kick Mr. Wrong
for breaking my heart."

UNKNOWN

Taking the Man Who Comes Along and Who Loves You

Life has a funny way of putting Mr. Right on your path. It's your job to recognize him. Women have often asked me how and where to find a man, and I've always said, "Take the first man who really, really loves you. He is the keeper."

It sounds as if this is not a powerful move, but I feel that, as far as love and romance go, a man who's crazy about you is a very smart move. You are a great catch. Right? A man who sees that is smart. A man who doesn't make you compete with other women for his love, who doesn't make you chase him all over town—that man is the keeper. A taken man or a man that you have to chase is a waste of your precious time.

Love, hot love, from a man who needs an erection is a good thing. Women are the receptacle of his love. He needs to feel the passion. Women need to receive this passion. A man crazy about you will be hot and full of passion.

The Absolute Woman

Many women think it's powerful to pursue a fabulous man that they are crazy about. I feel they are mistaken. I learned this when I was young from Elizabeth Taylor, as she only wanted the men who were crazy for her. God bless her for this important lesson.

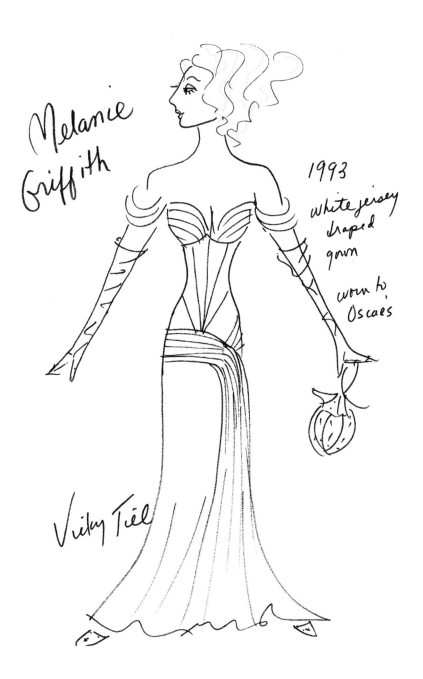

Melanie
Griffith

1993
white jersey
draped
gown

worn to
Oscars

Vicky Tiel

"I really don't need you."

MARILYN MONROE

Sex is a Two-Way Street!

Letting the male feel dominant is a problem for female bread-winners. For the first time since time began, many women are earning more money than their partners. Women in this century demanded equality, equal pay, and equal opportunity and now it is difficult putting female power into perspective with these higher accomplishments of the female over the male.

This is a huge problem that the successful female faces in life. Who decides what we do as a couple? Who decides who pays for what? Who decides where we live, who decides what we eat, how we decorate, what car to buy, how many children we have, whose mother we see for Sunday lunch?

These roles must be determined at the onset of any partnership; a relationship is no different. Yet, if women pay the majority of the bills and make all the decisions, a male can feel less than male and may eventually search for another mate who makes them feel more a male, as they need to get an erection and women don't. It's up to the female to get it up and keep it up. After thirty, it's never automatic. Women must create the excitement and stimulate the male brain as well as the penis. We can't fight biology; this is where smart women have it over "dumb babes" in the long run. Sex is mental stimulation with physical follow up, and the bed is where all the games are playable.

The greatest turn on is turning someone else on, especially someone you love. If a female is frigid and unable to come, it could be that she doesn't have the right partner. Any man in love should do what it takes to get his partner relaxed and orgasmic. If he's your mate, tell him what buttons to push: show and tell! Remember, sex is a part of nature, like eating and taking a poop. Everybody does it, like swimming, and once you learn, it's easy, and it's fun! Just jump in. Find a partner who helps you get it right, as no matter who the breadwinner is, a good sexual partner makes a good marriage.

Women must accept a power trade off and give the male his territory where he's dominant, besides in the bedroom. There are many territories where a man can easily dominate the decisions in the home, such as home building, home decor, home repair and gardening, car choices, school choices, vacation choices, even what TV shows he wants to watch. Let him watch sports on Sunday and you bake him cookies. I tell this to top female executives. Wear an apron and nothing else (very '40s) from time to time when the kids are away. Serve him cookies in bed. Keep your life together fun.

Also, I ASK MY MAN FOR HIS ADVICE ON EVERYTHING, ESPECIALLY CHILDREN, FAMILY, AND FRIENDS. It doesn't seem fair, but it is the trade off that the working man has given the stay-at-home mom in the past. Also, I LOVE ADVICE, as so many people know more than me.

I have never had a man earn more than me, except once, and he ended up cheating on me with a secretary who picked him up after work. His excuse when I found out was that "she loves to drive me everywhere." That was truly not my thing.

If you think this is not fair, just think of the female lion and how she lets the big hairy male growl and strut around like he's a big deal. Now, she's a cat! She kills food and drags it to him to eat first and then she eats it with her young. She knows there's a trade-off. Her male will kill himself protecting her and her cubs. He is her master, as he's bigger. These rules are constructed for nature, so why try to change nature? Instead, use nature like the female lion.

There is a southern way of suggesting something early on in the relationship and later the male thinks it's his idea. Females should not succumb to an ego problem of needing the world to know who's in charge. It doesn't matter, as long as you each get what you want. We want equality. The male feels he's made many of the decisions and the female gets what she wants most of the time.

I learned this from Nicky Haskell, a seventy-year-old LA hostess, who said, "I always say yes and always get what I want." Women want LOVE AND HAPPINESS AND, OF COURSE, GOOD SEX.

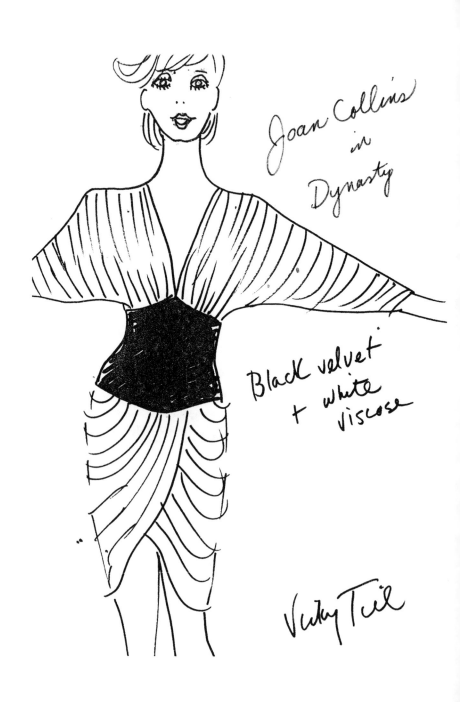

Joan Collins in Dynasty

Black velvet + white viscose

Vicky Teil

Vicky's list of No-No's

always say there are three ways to tell if a man is in love:

1. He wants to spend time with you.
2. He wants to spend his money on you.
3. He wants to have sex with you.

If you get two out of three, it's great!

Of course, after thirty years it's not that intense, but if you only get number three you are very lucky.

My No-No's on men. These are my ten "being in love with a great guy" deal breakers.

1. He hits you. It generally doesn't happen until after the first year, as men are on good behavior the first year to entice you, so don't marry any man until after the second year. Then you will see who they really are. My first husband took me to movies (which I loved) for the first year and then after that we never went again. He said he was in the movie business, so he didn't need to see them. The first year is all show. After the first year you must make boundaries and BOTH keep them.

2. He cheats and it's not a slip (a rare occasion); he cheats as a lifestyle.
3. He gambles all his money away.
4. He is a serious drug addict (not a pot smoker) or he's an alcoholic, as addiction will also take away all sexuality by midlife along with all his money and kindness.
5. He is a criminal, gangster, murderer, predator, Wall Street swindler, or a LIAR. Liars hide who they really are.
6. He lives in Afghanistan and you can only see him once a year.
7. He is insane by the DSM-5 Guide.
8. He is young enough to be your grandson. (I found that fifteen years younger is fine.)
9. He can't cook. (This is a deal breaker for me.) I love men who can cook. We all have our personal deal breaker.
10. He can't fix things (this is fine if you can fix things).

Prisilla Bresley wears the Mummy dress by Vicky Tiel

1989

"Smart women love smart men more
than smart men love smart women."

NATALIE PORTMAN

Internet Dating May Be Partially Responsible for the Rise in the Divorce Rate

I have interviewed my Parisian models who were looking for new boyfriends online and found that they were very satisfied with the results. Elle, a tall blond, went on three different websites after breaking up with a live-in boyfriend of several years. Her live-in boyfriend had not been Mr. Right but just Mr. Alright, and they broke up as she edged closer to wanting to be a mother. She needed Mr. Marriage Material. Elle lived in Neuilly, a posh Parisian suburb, large enough to find plenty of neighborhood men online.

When I asked Elle about online dating I was surprised that she knew about the pros and cons of this novel way (for my generation) of finding a husband.

Elle had been on about ten dates in ten months when she met Patrick online, her Mr. Right. Of those ten dates, only Patrick asked her to meet in the Louvre on their first date. He had planned to spend much of the day together, including inviting her to lunch. Of the other men, seven had asked her out, but only wanted to meet her in bars late at night, and only two men had asked her to meet them early in the day at coffee houses.

She had second and third dates with most of the ten men before Patrick, and had sex with a few, but, after sex most men moved on and never called her back, as they were basically using the site to meet women for sex. Patrick, wanting to spend time with her on their first date, proved he was looking for a real partner by sharing his love of art with his new lady. Elle was an artist as well as a model and Patrick was a journalist at Le Figaro, but he wanted to let Elle know that he wanted to please her. Patrick also wanted a deeper spiritual connection with a partner and wanted someone to share his beliefs as well as his time. After six months, they now spend all their time together and Patrick has her door key.

I have always told my girlfriends: Do not have the first date in a bar. My first *real* date with my first husband Ron was in a posh Paris hotel bar on the Rue du Bac. I was twenty-one and stupid, he was thirty-four and gorgeous, and he had been married twice. I had eleven cocktails with him that first date night and we closed the bar at 2:00 am. Of course, he was an alcoholic and he did his best to turn me into one as well. I can't complain as we had a wonderful life together living in London, Paris, and Rome. I learned a lot. We had two wonderful sons and way too much fun partying and seeing the world for most of our twenty-one years together, but when we divorced I quit drinking and looked for a non-drinking husband number two. I had crashed five cars, all European.

Internet dating is not the best way for a woman to meet a man today, mainly because men you meet online, total strangers, are often expecting sex on the first date. If you meet a new man in a bar and he drinks too much, he may have problems getting an erection. These internet sites have often become male sex parties and the men using them have no intention of finding a life partner.

A woman looking for a true companion, and not a party boy, may misunderstand that this "only so-so sex act" on the first date was because the man was not physically attracted to her or that this male has problems with erections. Either way, the new lifestyle of internet porn addiction may have ruined any realistic sexual expectations on both people's part, mainly due to the specialized camerawork and excellent sex directors on these internet porn films that are way too perfect to be real.

I do recommend meeting a future partner in person, with the vibes floating back and forth, as I believe your life partner will be put in your path by higher powers and it's your job to recognize him.

However, I do not believe that having sex on your first date is a bad thing, as I had sex with both my husbands the day I met them. My first husband, Hollywood Ron met me (the day before our first date) in the cafeteria in the Studios de Billancourt in Paris, while I was on my first job doing the costumes for an American film, *What's New Pussycat?* Ron was doing Elizabeth Taylor's makeup for *Sandpiper,* and he asked me right away at my lunch table for my phone number and my address in Paris. I was surprised "like crazy" when he showed up that very same evening at my front door, while I was getting ready for bed. We had sex right then and there in the hallway, and continued into the bedroom and had sex over and over all through the night, and that love and attraction lasted for twenty-one years. I was his third wife and, sadly, I caught him cheating frequently after we had our two kids and happily I moved on.

For my second husband, I found a much younger fisherman in Key West Florida while renting his boat. Magic Mike was twenty-nine and I was forty-three, and after spending a day shark fishing at sea on the Gulf, we had dinner and went directly to a motel opposite the Garrison Bight Dock. We trashed it and amazingly that good sex has lasted for thirty-one years.

So, I am totally for meeting Mr. Right and jumping right into bed with him. But, I fall in love at first sight, which is impossible on a machine. We don't even know if the photo online is twenty years old, or if it's even him!

Go to your favorite busy gas station! It's full of cute men.

Anna Nicole
Smith
wedding

Bourdon ecru
lace
corset top

ivory jersy
and lace
gown.

Vicky Tiel

"A kiss is a rosy dot
over the 'i' of loving."

CYRANO DE BERGERAC

Finding Someone to Love and Not Online

Men you can actually see are all over the place: Planes, trains, buses, airports, cruises, baseball games (where you can move seats), walking down the street, grocery stores, casual restaurants, and even the beach or fishing (if you hire cute fishing boat captains).

Men are all around you. Here are some tips to help you find one!

1. **Sports:** If you want to know where most women find men, it's usually somewhere sports-related. If you talk to a single, available man, sparks can fly. Each one of these places below are places where my clients found their husbands. Besides the gym or the golf course try:

   * Hiking in Alaska
   * Ski cable cars in Switzerland or Aspen
   * Beverly Hills Kickboxing Class
   * Safari in Africa

* Madison Square Garden in New York (go alone and sit next to a group of men)
* Fishing in Key West (where I met my second husband)
* Go to your local Bass Pro Shop and talk to men buying fishing poles

2. **Grocery stores:** Not only will you find a neighbor to date but you can see what he likes to eat before you flirt.

3. **Churches, funerals, weddings, yoga, or meditation centers:** Spiritual retreats are for people in transformations, sometimes break ups. The ashram is the gym/church for the spiritual crowd.

4. **Gas stations:** I used to talk to all the single men about my car problems. I would ask them, "Are my tires okay?" or "I don't understand if I'm out of water?" Something like that. Get a coffee with them and chat.

5. **High school reunions:** The actor George Segal remarried his high school girlfriend!

6. **Art galleries:** Talk to the single men about art comparisons, "What do you think..."

7. **Bloomingdale's men's department:** Ask a single man if he likes this tie for your brother, for example.

8. **Dining:** Get seated near a solo man who, seeing your big smile, comes over to chat. In France, our outdoor cafes are known as the best pick-up places. Just smile. It's a national pastime to spend half a day in a café making friends.

9. **The workplace:** Movie stars fall in love on set all the time. I hear Mika and Joe on MSNBC are a couple now. Just don't go for your married boss.

10. **Schools:** Go back to school and take a class, you might meet a guy with similar interests.
11. **Walking your dog:** It can be in a park or in the city. Who can resist a cute dog?

The best state to meet a man is Alaska. Take a drive out of Anchorage to Fairbanks with a friend and hit the cafés in Eagle River. There are at least twenty single men sitting alone every day.

The best city to meet a man is Pensacola, Florida, as there are some 200,000 military men on the Gulf Coast; the commanders are there for the airports and the retired military moved there to stay together.

The best place to find a millionaire is at the Hotel de Paris for the Grand Prix of Monaco. But, I'd rather make my own money. I actually wear a Grand Prix of Monaco cap on all my travels that I bought myself.

The second best place to find a millionaire is an African safari. Go alone. Generally men go there who have gotten divorced to get on with their lives. Visit Namibia, it's safe and chic. Brad and Angelina went there on their honeymoon.

The worst place to find a husband is at a bar, as you mainly find alcoholics.

My best advice for a first date is to *listen. Do not talk too much.* Don't exaggerate or discuss politics, as strong opinions turn off men. We need to find out who they are, as they tell you things on the first date that they may choose to hide later on.

But always remember, happiness is a warm puppy. If you can't get a man, get a puppy!

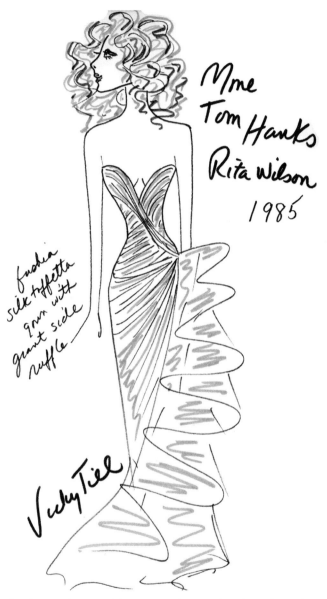

Mme
Tom Hanks
Rita Wilson
1985

fushia
silk taffetta
gown with
giant sickle
ruffle

Vicky Tiel

This is the dress I designed for Rita Wilson on her first "big" date with Tom Hanks.

"French girls still have the Jane Birkin culture. You can go just like that, without makeup, without managing your hair."

EMMANUELLE ALT

Forever Young

As an artist, I must stay young. "Forever Young" is what my fellow artist, Bob Dylan, sang to all of us in the '60s, and we sure did try.

As a young fashion designer, I learned to hang out with my models, and they were often my besties. Today, at seventy-four, not much has changed. When I live in the city, I still hang with the models, the stylists, and my fellow artists. In the countryside, I hang out with the daughters of my neighbors, as their moms are often not in the same time/age zone as me.

One way to stay young is to follow pop music, and of course our pop crushes, so I have to admit that I bought the entire Justin Bieber H&M leisure collection and the Miley Cyrus Collection, which she created for Walmart when she was only sixteen.

I was not surprised to read the recent report by Tara Bahrampour in *The Washington Post* about the sex life of today's teenagers and millennials. It seems that young people have fifteen percent less sex than their parents, and the reason they have less sex as couples is that they have sex with themselves while watching porn on the internet. The percentage of teens who do not have sex before eighteen has gone from eight percent, during their parents' teen years, to fifteen percent of teens today. It has doubled!

In Japan, the population and birth rate has plummeted due to internet porn. They have 300,000 less people, with a population of 125 million, where the U.S. is not watching as much porn and has had an increase of 2.2 million with a population of 323 million.

I recently had lunch with a girlfriend in New York who, at thirty-three, is leaving her husband because he's a masturbating, computer-porn addict. He prefers sex alone. Is this the future? Will women be searching for unique men who like to touch a real body? With all her "Boudoir fashion efforts" and all my Hollywood advice, nothing could make her young husband give up his love affair with his hand.

The internet has also changed how we manage our relationships. I have another friend in Paris who is thirty-four; she had an ex-husband, her best lover ever, who wanted her back and begged her to divorce her current husband, the father of her two children (who is also having less sex with her due to masturbating while watching his beloved internet porn). This girlfriend, tired of using sex toys like the G spot Rabbit, instead of hiring a detective, created a fake sexy female persona on the internet and contacted each of the two husbands with sexy photos, waiting to trap them. Her first husband responded with a photo of his penis and wanted a hook up. Her current husband said, "I am married and not interested." She stayed with him, of course, and they are doing sexual counseling which is working.

Tara Bahrampour has been writing about sex and the millennials for the last few years and her articles really resonate.

I've been writing on my blog that seventy is the new forty-five, as my mom and dad recently died at ninety-five and ninety-seven. So we are living twenty years longer than when I was young in the '60s, and there's a good chance I'll live to be 105–110.

This means that everything we do in our life today is as if we are twenty years younger. This also means we have to plan our life from sixty-five to 100.

Sixty is the new forty.

Fifty is the new thirty.

Thirty is the new seventeen.

Tara claims that female teens of fourteen and on are even getting plastic surgery to be more like their reality TV stars, and doing it for their own self-satisfaction, not to seduce boys. So, these females are having less sex for fear of emotional involvement and "losing control," which often leads to anorexia and bulimia. Fear of losing control of one's emotions (another topic of our times) also leads to the need for antidepressants, and that leads to loss of libido, therefore less sex.

Because we are living longer, everything is delayed, therefore real romance and marriages are postponed as long as possible. They are now replaced with texting, sexting, pornos, and self-sexual satisfaction.

Fear of pregnancy and disease has made thirty the new seventeen.

It's safer to delay being an adult today.

Stats from the *Journal of Child Development*

* Adolescents who have a driver's license went from 86 percent in 1976 to 63 percent today.
* Adolescents who work went from 75 percent in 1976 to 55 percent today.
* Adolescents who drink went from 93 percent in 1976 to 67 percent today.
* Adolescents who have sex went from 54 percent in 1976 to 41 percent today.

Paula Prentiss in "What's New Pussycat" 1964

gold lame silk print

Bra and hip hugging mini skirt

pink maribou boa

dance scene with Peter O'Toole at Castel's Disco

bedroom mules for shoes

Vicky Tiel

"I did everything he did backwards,
and in high heels."

GINGER ROGERS

Sexism Is the Topic of Our Times

Having sex with a man you don't desire is one of the reasons why women have lost power from 2500 BC until today.

Why women have sex with men they don't desire:

1. if they want to gain a better position in society
2. if they want to get help with their career
3. if they want to get a financial reward
4. if their family has chosen someone for them
5. if the person was famous
6. if they are feeling bad about themselves and want to feel better

The President of the United States has been caught on tape saying that if you're famous you can do anything. The presidents of many companies all think and do the same. They feel they are entitled and that free sex comes with the paycheck. The heads of networks, movie companies, and Congress, have all been dropping out one by one because 2017 became the year of the unexpected sexual awakening. Why now? Why 2017? There has been a definite cultural shift. I attribute it to the internet. It has completely changed shopping, and sex is right up there with shopping in terms of importance to women.

Well, surprise surprise to the men of today. IT IS ALL OVER. The internet and modern technology have changed the women you harassed for 4,500 years and I say it's about time. Conversations can be taped, smart phones capture everything, and SMART young women, even in Arab countries, want to drive and be free to go and do whatever they want. And they will. Sooner than later.

I remember being twenty-three in 1966 and going to the George V Hotel in Paris with my beautiful partner, Mia Fonssagrives, to interview a world-famous producer for a costume design job. He was being massaged by Fred, the infamous masseur of the movie stars (and thought to be the masseur of Hitler). The much older producer was naked on a table under a plush, white, monogrammed towel. "Come here," he said to us, "I want to see you gorgeous creatures. Take off your clothes."

I responded accordingly, Mia hesitated. As I stood in my Mia-Vicky French lace underwear with both Double D's pointed at him, he admiringly turned to a bewildered Mia and said, "But ladies I must see you both fully unclothed." I did not feel dumb, as I thought I was selling our new French lingerie line for the film, but I was stunned to hear he wanted us naked!

Mia, a year older and used to being unimpressed by famous men as her stepfather was Irving Penn, the *Vogue* photographer, said to the naked producer, "We don't need to be naked as we are the costume designers, but you can see we can do great French bikinis," pointing to my body. He was taken aback as he thought we were up for the actress's role, eventually awarded to Claudine Auger. We wondered and guessed what all the James Bond actresses had to do for their parts.

Yes, we still got the job of designing the swimwear for the film, and the photo on Claudine Auger in our Diamond Thong Bikini made a full color page in *Look* magazine. And yes, we made our own money. Lots of money.

In the movie and fashion industry especially, this was a common issue. For the movie *Candy*, which was shot in Rome, the director and the producer had both promised their young Candy candidate the starring role. So, who would win? Which mistress would get the part of Candy? Of course, the money man won. The Italian producer won and his sweetie became Candy, although she was Swedish and she barely spoke English.

But what about the young women who are in fear of losing their jobs? Women of today (after the outing of The Bad Boys in 2017) do have a leg up, as men now have to think twice before harassing women in the workplace.

Having worked on sixteen movies and having met the heads of all the major movie studios, fashion conglomerates, and the world's largest companies, as I dressed their wives and met the husbands while at the balls or seated in my shop, I personally feel that the vulgar men who grab your crotch are the minority. These pathetic "rapists" are insecure because they were not hot or popular as teenagers, and were probably not well hung. They think that they can now at midlife make up for their "loser" childhood insecurity with their wealth and power as older men. Yet, these men are still losers. Powerful women recognize this fact and do not become their quiet victims.

Today these men are being outed in America and it's quite a turn of events.

Perhaps more women will learn to say "No more."

Of course, in France, we know the difference between flirting and harassment. French women flirt, it's true, and sexuality is viewed differently. The French are rarely shocked. In France, our President Mitterrand kept a second family for fourteen years with a daughter Mazarine, but he stayed with his official wife on Rue de Bièvre in Paris. (Both wives went together to his funeral.) Today our President Macron is married to his twenty-four-year-older high school teacher.

I love this quote from Mary Russell, a fashion editor of *American Vogue* in France since the '60s and still living there. Mary told me "I've been known to flirt outrageously with the famous and the infamous. IT'S ALL ABOUT MUTUAL CONSENT. Flirting is a way of life for all ages, all sexes, it certainly is not dead here in France."

Yes, flirting is fine when it's mutual. Women must learn to send the message that it's mutual and learn how to flirt by watching lots of French movies.

Women must not let men humiliate us, no matter who they are. We are not for sale. The mindset of men since 2500 BC, that we are objects for sale, is over.

No man ever made a grab at Cleopatra/Elizabeth Taylor. Ever! She chose.

Now women will all learn to choose. It's easy, tell the men when they make unwanted passes, "I CHOOSE."

TELL ALL YOUR GIRLFRIENDS THIS. PRINT IT ON YOUR T-SHIRTS, "I CHOOSE."

Let's start a movement.

I CHOOSE.

Claudine
Anget
1965
costume from
James Bond film
"Thunderball"
publicity shot
Look magazine

diamond trim
on black jersey

Vicky Tiel

"A woman can run faster
with her skirt up than a man can
with his pants down."

MY SOUTHERN HUSBAND, MIKE HAMILTON

How to say "NO" and say "I CHOOSE"

Saying "no" to a powerful man is a technique I've perfected. I have yet to have sex with a man I did not desire, although I did have six men who tried to rape me, all of them famous. They all failed, including my my girlfriend's husband, a handsome designer who invaded my bathing by coming into the shower naked while I stayed at their beachfront mansion. She divorced him, but sexy, roving, rich husbands were a popular '80s thing.

I've had my nipples tweaked twice, wearing sexy, Vicky lace dresses. The first time was at twenty-two by one of the titans of 7th Avenue, who was hiring the top European prêt-à-porter designers to bring their youthful styles to create an American-European brand. When I said "I'm going with a rock star," he left me alone. He still gave me the designer job. The second time happened when I met with a prominent man in the beauty business to license my first perfume. His company did not carry my perfume after I turned down the man's advances.

Men with power that can help you and advance your career know this, and they prey on women who desperately want to be famous. THESE PREDATORS KNOW YOU NEED THEIR HELP AND PRESUME YOU CANNOT SAY NO!

However, they can be turned down when they come on to you with a simple phrase..."I CHOOSE."

If you want to be funny and light about it, if you are sure you are in no danger, say:

"DARLING, I AM WITH A MAN WHO IS CONNECTED SO YOU BETTER NOT TRY ANYTHING."

If you want to be serious and officious, say:

"WHAT EXACTLY DOES THIS HAVE TO DO WITH MY JOB?"

If you don't show fear, the balance of power is shifted.

If the classic approach in telling a man in heat that you are with someone and not interested does not work, and this aggressor continues to chase you and undress, which means that any job you get comes with contingencies, just say this, "DARLING, I ONLY GO WITH GORGEOUS STUDS THAT I CHOOSE." That will shut him up and put him in his place, as great studs don't rape, they have lines of women waiting for repeats.

When you make your own money, you don't need these men. When you make your own money and when you have your own personal power, it smells! It comes out of your pores. When you have your own money, not your husband's, not your father's, you are Feminine Power!

1969, Mia and I in New York just before Mia left Paris to become a sculptress. The dress I'm wearing I made again for HSN in 2011. I love timeless fashion.

"Any girl can be glamorous.
All you have to do is stand still
and look stupid."

HEDY LAMARR

How to Pull Any Guy You Want: the "Nathalie Delon Technique"

Sometime in the late '60s when Mia, my fashion partner and best friend, moved out and married couturier, Louis Feraud, I began to hang out with Nathalie Delon.

Nathalie, a French actress, was the young girl who broke up the engagement and the future marriage of France's leading man, Alain Delon, and Europe's superstar, Romy Schneider, in the early '60s. Nathalie and Alain, after their short marriage and a beautiful son, both moved on to break the hearts of multiple celebrities. After breaking the heart of France's best-looking actor, Nathalie ran off with Louis Malle, France's best-looking film director and later lived for years with the world's best-looking music producer on an island in the Bahamas.

Nathalie was a slim blond with perfect pointy breasts, and I was a curvy brunette with double D's. Perfect mates. We would dine late and do the Paris clubs, and it was Nathalie who taught me how to pull in any man you want.

I was reading Keith Richards' biography, *Life*, and there is Nathalie running through multiple chapters, everyone in love with her, breaking celebrity hearts and moving on.

Nathalie was involved with Richard Burton during the filming of *Bluebeard* in the late 1970s, when Elizabeth left Burton over his fling with Sophia Loren, but Nat wasn't someone who liked to share.

Nat and I were both party animals, dancing at Castel's and finding gorgeous men to take home to her sumptuous apartment on the Place des Invalides overlooking the city. Her method to getting all the men she wanted was simple. She taught me her trick.

This is only for eighteen to thirty-five-year-olds who are sexy/powerful and know it.

1. Walk into the most trendy club in the city wearing something so hot men will melt. (For Nathalie, that was slinky, silver satin pants and a see-thru chiffon tailored shirt. For me, it was a sexy lace mini dress with a bra top and my boobs peeking out.)
2. Hold your drink in one hand and eyeball the room until you find a target, then flash your best asset. (For Nat it was her perfect face and killer smile, for me, I'd eyeball my boobs, then look up and stare at him.)
3. Then you POINT YOUR FINGER UP AND CURL IT AND BECKON HIM TO COME. HE WILL.

The Nathalie Delon technique is perfect for ANYWHERE: in the supermarket, the gas station, the café on the corner, at a wedding, or a barbecue. It works if you are looking your best and you have a great big gorgeous smile on your face when you curl that finger.

A tres chic American dress designer Susie L. was visiting Paris and crossed the street next to the Café Flore when she smiled at a passing man, wagged her finger, and found a Frenchman, the love of her life.

Come here you cutie ♡

Nathalie
Delon

1971

Costume "Bluebeard" film
white jersey
diamond straps, white
fur boa

slit front

Vicky Tiel

"Marriage is simple, your wife does whatever she wants and you do whatever she wants."

WRITTEN ON THE WALL OF A RESTAURANT IN ALABAMA

Which Marriage (or Relationship) Type Are You?

There are two types of marriages: the piggyback marriage and the marriage of two people side by side, who are each on separate paths due to their work and travel. Side-by-siders can't piggyback; their paths can separate, often by very wide distances, and then suddenly they flow back together. I know, I'm one of them.

My two husbands never phoned or (texted) five times a day, or even twice. My girlfriends in their thirties text their men all day long. They will be piggybackers until they break up with a partner and then will piggyback again with their next men. It's proof of love. The nonstop texting has drastically changed the world for the side-by-sider!

My mother and stepfather never spent a night apart in their sixty-year marriage. My stepdad called Mom when he got to work at the Treasury building in Washington. He died at Christmas time and my mother had a stroke when she saw his empty bed. Just like in the incredible film *Amour*, where Jean Louis Trintignant, Brigitte Bardot's amour and the man she started the sexual revolution with, now elderly, portrays the piggyback husband putting his wife, who had a stroke, to bed each night, tenderly tucking the covers under her chin.

My best friend in Paris, Christine Lambert, was a fabulous decorator and was married to the handsome writer and film critic, Gilles Lambert, who was sixteen years her senior, for almost fifty years. When Gilles died of cancer at eighty-three, Christine immediately got brain cancer at sixty-seven and died in months calling his name, "Gillou."

On the other hand, side-by-side marriages are two people following two paths, sometimes separated for work or travel and coming together without any bitterness but with the same goal: to remain independent, yet remain a couple.

My real dad's marriage to Mom was only long enough to have me and enough time for Mom to spend money from his bank account to buy some expensive shoes. Dad never remarried, as having a piggyback wife, and having a piggyback bank account was not his thing. He spent his retirement years single, with girlfriends, cruising the world, and Mom married a U.S. tax boss who adored all her shoes.

Would you turn down a film shoot in Morocco because you can't leave your man? Can you be a half or must you be a whole? Do you love to have the five phone calls or five texts a day, and need a man who wants the same? Do you panic if he stops texting?

I remember the day when my husband number two said he was done with driving me to the Miami airport from our home in Key West. I traveled all the time, as I also lived in Paris. I understood. I am used to myself and my work and my travel and can't be dependent on a phone call from anyone! I am not unique, all actors, movie people, artists, gallery owners, musicians, all fashion, all military, all truck drivers, and the boating and fishing and airline industry, all these millions of people are better off with a side by side partner.

I have noticed now in my seventies that the human being in general is also a side-by-sider or a piggybacker in their relationships with their life-long friends. The side-by-sider can live alone in the woods for weeks like myself writing a book, calling a friend or two each day, or they can travel the world on a bicycle. The piggybacker needs to socialize, needs lunches and dinners and clubs, or needs organized communal activities.

They cannot live alone.

You must choose early in life which marriage or life partner type you are.

"Love yourself first and everything
else falls into line.
You really have to love yourself
to get anything done in this world."

LUCILLE BALL

Turning Forty-Three

Turning forty-three was the beginning of my new life, the end of my first marriage, and suddenly reality set in. I wanted real conversations, real connections, less parties in palaces and museums and waiting for the big next party. Would I fly to Monte Carlo this weekend for the Grand Prix and Cannes? I had nannies and drivers and could leave as I pleased but I was forty-three.

Reality set in: real conversations, real connections, real people.

"What will I wear," would no longer be my mantra.

Life had been a pretty picture in the fashion magazines, me posed with my glamorous make-up man husband—who would paint my face and photograph me—his vision of his wife to present to the world in our perfect Normandy country home, with baby-blue Easter eggs hidden under the weeping willow tree.

Underneath the facade was a happy artist but a sad soul. Not only did I have a cheating husband, but I had to look forward, from being the most photographed woman in the room to just another forty-year-old in a crowd of older women, drinking champagne at posh parties and discussing top plastic surgeons. There had to be more.

I made a list of what made me happy and what did not.

Midlife is a time to examine who we are.

My list (with ten being the best) was:

* Work: 10
* Friends: 6
* Children: 9
* Health: 10
* Food: 10
* Homes: 10
* Income: 10
* Husband: 2 or a 3
* Sex: 0, as he had cheated so much I didn't want him to touch me and AIDS made me afraid as well.

The crazy '60s and '70s were over, and even Warren Beatty stopped sleeping with four girls a day and became a faithful husband.

Joy Philbin

draped
jersey gown
and Bolero
gown "Sade"
with
hip drape

worn on her
daughter's wedding
day 2005

Vicky Tiel

*"Be yourself,
everyone else is already taken."*

ZARA WINDOW ON FIFTH AVE IN NEW YORK

My Point of View

I am not deep, I do not think about or retain bad things. I do not suffer, I am not in denial, I'm always that way.

I search for visual pleasure: in nature, in art, in books, songs, ballet, TV, movies, in my pets, in my friends, ANYTHING that is positive and pleasurable. I must eat great food.

If a bad thing happens, I think it happened for a reason, that it happened for a lesson and it will lead to good thing that will happen afterwards, and I will learn why the bad thing happened so I can grow and be even happier. I had two miscarriages and a sad divorce but nothing happened to diminish my happy thoughts, every day of my life has always been a joy.

To verify this point that I must not be deep, that it's just my magical thinking, I had to be sure, so I called my closest high school girlfriend, Jan Tupper Kearney in Oakland, California and asked her if I was as insensitive and powerful as I remembered. She said it was true, I was not sensitive at all. Nothing got to me.

I recall trying out in the eighth grade for junior high school cheerleader and getting my period, a spot of fresh red blood the size of an apple in the dead center on the back of my white pleated skirt. It happened just before it was my turn to try out in the school gym. I didn't panic, I thought God did this to make me flip faster, so no one will see the blood, as the jury was seated in chairs directly in front.

I flipped so fast I got voted first, right after I tried out. I was a cheerleader for the next four years through both junior high and high school.

Being yourself is not as easy as it may seem. All of us are subject to the expectations of society and of our families. How we feel about this, the decisions we make, are what makes us different, it's what makes us, well, us!

I've always wondered if I was reincarnated. I have thought maybe it's possible I have lived before and was a tranquil male monk and now I'm a female, here to play dress up and have fun, but I must still teach happiness.

Bianca
Jagger

wedding
ST Tropez

White silk
"Marilyn"
gown
green penny
size dots.

Vicky Tiel

"My mom said to me, 'You know sweetheart one day you should settle down and marry a rich man.'
I said, 'Mom, I am a rich man.'"

CHER

Billionaires

"Marry me," said the male billionaire to the pop singer.

The latest trend in celebrity weddings is to marry a male billionaire.

Jerry Hall just married Rupert Murdoch and Serena Williams just married Alexis Ohanian.

I have dressed billionaire wives (including royalty) all my career and have concluded one thing: if the woman is not equally self-made, the male will eventually turn her into a secretary, or a driver, or both. Donald Trump divorced Ivana when she became the official decorator of Trump Hotels, with an office and a staff in The Trump Tower.

The happiest women I knew who were mega-rich were all self-made.

Coco Chanel, Elizabeth Taylor, Brigitte Bardot, Jane Birkin, Joan and Jackie Collins, Sherry Lansing, Edith Head, Diana Vreeland, Oprah Winfrey, and Joyce Ma, the Chinese fashion mogul. They often married financial equals, but to assure their power they paid their own way and let everybody know it.

The billionaire is just not used to anyone *not* obeying his orders. You need to jump. Their behavior can be monitored for

Above: Creating my first original perfume in a crystal bottle with a sculpted lady stopper, 1989. It is now in the perfume museum in Grasce, France.

Left: 1971, my ring draped dress in the first fashion show without my partner Mia. These timeless dresses are forever—Jennifer Lawrence wore a knockoff of this in her movie, American Hustle.

Above: My 2nd husband Mike (on the left) on our Vicky Tiel boat in Key West in 1988.

Left: My first husband "Hollywood Ron" Berkeley, the great make-up man, at our riverfront island home in Normandy, France.

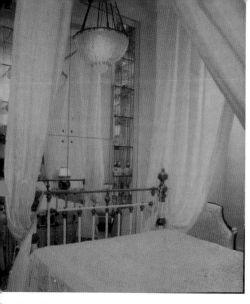

Clockwise from above:

In my couture salon at Bergdorf Goodman in the 80s.

My antique brass Paris bed that I've owned all my life in France, and a Lalique lamp.

Model Barbara and I in my dress salon at Bergdorf Goodman.

Vicky and Mia Fonssagrives start the mini in Paris, 1964. We wore it with a long coat.

Below, top: At work on the show of my collection with sketches of how the models will line up.

Bottom: Mia and I started selling the first jumpsuits in our Paris shop in 1968.

op: My Paris shop at 21 Rue Bonaparte, 1971. he model is Clementine Ettori; she was my tepson's girlfriend. Her sister was Elizabeth aylor's hairdresser.

ottom: My Vogue ad shot by husband Ron erkeley.

Vicky Tiel creates timeless fashions from 1968 to 2011.

More timeless fashions from 1971 to 2011.

Right: Ulysse—my men's fragrance bottle. The design was created from a Greek frieze. It has sold nonstop since 1998.

Below: The magic ostrich feather was sent from heaven in 2011 by Elizabeth Taylor and landed on my New York mountain cabin deck. It was the color of my first perfume bottles. She was telling me that I could sell perfume on TV.

Bottom: In 1989, I created the Vicky Tiel perfume business, sculpting my first bottles in Paris with Pierre Dinand. He gave me the sculpting tools and I did them myself.

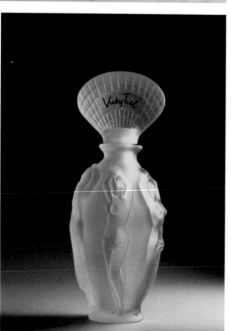

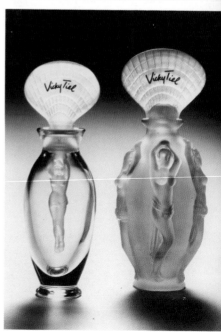

Top: Richard Burton and Virna Lisi in my gown for the film BlueBeard *shot in Budapest.*

Bottom: Lying on the bank of our Normandy mill house.

Right: Ladies' night at a plantation in Natchez, Mississippi. The theme was "Gone with the Wind" and I wore a see-through lace top.

Below: On our fishing boat, the Vicky Tiel, in Key West, 1988.

I still own this apartment in Paris on the Seine riverbank, where I raised my children.

*op, right: In Positano, Italy, the city of
ove, where I lived on weekends with my
rst husband Ron Berkeley while shooting
Rome with the Burtons for 3 years.*

*ottom: In Athens, Greece at the Parthenon,
efore filming* Oedipus Rex *with Orson
Velles and Christopher Plummer.*

Clockwise from above:

Tony Randall and wife in my gown.

With Roger Verger, chef of Moulin de Mougins, the top restaurant in the south of France.

I created the bridal department at Bergdorf Goodman and did international wedding dresses. This bride was in Switzerland.

Clockwise from below:

My wedding in London to Ron Berkeley.

Marriage to Mike Hamilton, on our Florida farm riverbank in 1996. I'm wearing Ivana Trump's returned pink wedding suit.

Wearing the first see-through top at the ladies' plantation party in 1999, many years before it became acceptable.

Clockwise from right:

"Girlfriends Talk" with Elizabeth Taylor at my wedding to her makeup man, Hollywood Ron.

Elizabeth Taylor and I at the relaunch of our shop in Paris, now called Vicky Tiel, wearing my first hot pants.

In Monte Carlo on a yacht, in May at the Grand Prix of Monaco, doing the costumes for the movie Grand Prix.

Clockwise from left:

With Jimmy Rowe, my first steady boyfriend at age 14.

My childhood home in Chevy Chase, Maryland, practicing to be a cheerleader for Kensington Junior High at age 13.

Mrs. Clint (Maggie) Eastwood and son Kyle at their home in Big Sur, California.

Right: My Brazilian model Luana, who became the Duchess of Noailles. The Duke fell in love with her in this dress.

Clockwise from below:

My poodle Trippy on the French pillow from my Highgate Manor bedding collection for HSN.

At home in Paris in 1989, on my French brass bed when M Mike moved in.

Feeding my adorable chickens in vintage French fashion. We have a 40 acre riverfront farm in a Florida wilderness park with well water, and we grow our own food.

*Me at 74, in Justin Bieber pants and a
Vicky top, at Frenchy's on Clearwater
Beach, my hangout when I work on TV.*

a courtship, but in the long run most of them respond best to women who act like high-class whores.

For women with true understanding of their Feminine Power, I recommend for them to stay the breadwinner and find a cool guy who doesn't mind. Generally, very, very intelligent men are not good with making money and they are great partners, also athletes, home builders, teachers, farmers, and fishermen. "You complete me!" That is the goal. Find a true partner not a competitor.

Elizabeth Taylor 1990

white beaded lace gown lined in tulle with draped jersey skirt worn for engagement party

worn with matching purse

VickyTel

"Thou had made me endless,
such is thy pleasure. This frail
vessel thou emptiest again and again,
and fillest it ever with fresh life."

RABINDRANATH TAGORE

Sex Over Sixty

I must admit that if you mate or marry with the sexual love of your life and if you are a ten and he is a ten (not a two), and if he is in good health and not an alcoholic, his love stick works just fine, if not perfectly. As your life is less hectic and you have more free time after sixty, I can assure women that nothing changes sexually over sixty. You know exactly what each other likes and you become a SEXPERT for each other.

My mom and stepdad moved into our Florida farm and they had the bedroom at the end of the hall. One morning after breakfast I tried to enter the room without knocking only to hear my stepdad say, "don't come in, we're having sex." With that, he slammed the door closed. They were having stand-up sex by the door. They were ninety-three and ninety-five. I mentioned this to the nurse and she said that was their favorite spot.

Of course, dad was a non-drinker. My experience has been that my heavy drinking first husband had erection problems in midlife and often cheated, as a new woman was always a thrill for the first few times, which he later confessed during our divorce.

Aretha
Franklin

worn for honors
at Kennedy Center
1997

green duchesse satin
gown with train and
large cape

Vicky Tiel

"When love rules,
power disappears.
When power rules,
love disappears."

PAULO COELHO

Having It All

The discussion of *having it all* is the most important intimate conversation of our times for women. Marissa Mayer, then the pregnant CEO of Yahoo, and Anne-Marie Slaughter, of the *Atlantic* article "Why Women Still Can't Have It All," were on opposite sides of the discussion. Women, power, and "having it all" is a subject that needs resolution for all women today in modern countries.

I am of the opinion, as is Marissa Mayer, that having it all is very possible today, especially for the women under forty. Men and women may have different bodies, but equal hearts and minds, and deserve equal respect and equal opportunity. I feel Professor Slaughter made a mistake when working out the details on her side of the argument. She took a job in a city she did not live in. If she were totally committed to her government job, she should have moved to Washington. She also had a child who needed special attention. That is not the case for all families, as my two French sons could not wait for me to fly to New York so they could throw sleep over parties.

Just because a woman gives birth does not mean she has to stop work. In the Paris fashion world, we have four collections a year; unlike any other industry in the arts, fashion folk cannot delay these dates for pregnancy, illness, or even death. The collection goes on.

My company presented dress collections for forty-eight years without skipping a beat. How? I'm not superwoman or super rich. I had good employees that I paid well. I love my work. I help women and design the dress they wear on the most important day of their lives. The photos of them in my dress are on their mantle until they die. (Many tell me that they will never sell or give away my gown.)

When I was pregnant at thirty-three at the end of October during Paris Fashion Week, I held my baby inside my body and willed him to not "pop" out. My cooperative son stayed put until November 4. Once he was cleaned up and dressed in Baby Dior, he bonded with me for some cuddle time and then we headed over to our fashion showroom with his nanny to help his mama sell gowns. Today he organizes the filming of multinational movies.

Stats on Women at Work in 2015

* Today, 34 percent of women have BAs, and only 26 percent of men. Women are getting more BAs than men.
* In 1970, only 11.2 percent of women in the work force had college degrees. Today, 40 percent of women in the work force have college degrees.
* Women get more college degrees than men, but earn 83 percent of the income of men for the same job.
* In 1970, 62 percent of women worked. Today, 83 percent of women work.
* In 1970, 27 percent of wives contributed to the family income. In 2015, 37 percent of wives contributed.
* Four places where women earn more than men today: Connecticut, Vermont, Washington D.C., Rhode Island.
* Places with the widest gap between men's pay and women's pay: Lousiana, Alabama, Oklahoma, West Virginia, Iowa.
* 42 percent of women are the sole breadwinners for families.
* In 2017, 38 percent of women earned more than their husbands, up four times since the 1960s.
* 53 percent of women have multiple jobs, and 45 percent of men have multiple jobs.
* Today, women work an average of 35.9 hours. Men work an average of 41 hours a week.
* Today 61 percent of women work full time, as compared to 41 percent in 1970.
* Today, women own over ten million businesses!

* Only 4 percent of women earn more on software jobs. An amazing stat—the tech male wants a private boys club!
* Sadly, only 13 percent of female artists are represented in museums or galleries.
* The women of the millennial generation are now worried about getting divorced if they earn more than their husbands, or partners, so many are not getting married.

*"I leave before being left.
I decide."*

BRIGITTE BARDOT

Happiness Is a Choice

The Dalai Lama says "The very purpose of life is to be happy." The Beatles sing "Happiness Is A Warm Gun"—or a warm puppy, or a warm meal, or warm love.

We wake up each day with a choice: what to say, what to do, where to work, where to live, who to love, what to wear, buy, eat, drink. What to put in and on our bodies?

I CHOOSE HAPPINESS. I CHOOSE EVERYTHING THAT PROMOTES IT AND REJECT WHATEVER CAUSES UNHAPPINESS. HAPPINESS = GOOD HEALTH.

My Chinese herbal doctor in New York, who has been my doctor for twenty-five years, George Y.C. Wong (a cancer specialist), says unhappiness can be the main cause of cancer. It's the body committing suicide.

I choose to accept the bad times and look for a silver lining in the bad thing. Pain is a good thing, it teaches me how to ignore the negative. Life is a lesson. The lesson is love and compassion and acceptance. The lesson is that everything happens for a reason, everything happens for the best, and with patience we will eventually find out what the best is awaiting us down the road.

After twenty-one years in Paris and Normandy, my marriage fell apart, we divorced and I lost my beautiful mill house, but I found a better, younger husband for growing old with, a bigger home for my books and my art and with more land to grow our own food, and a bigger river to swim in year-round and not only in the summer.

Always remember this: The best is awaiting us down the road. Be patient. Always smile.

Brigitte
Bardot

Irrisistable
early
1970's

VickyTiel

"There is a shade of red
for every woman."

AUDREY HEPBURN

When I Needed to Find a New Husband, I Put On a Red Dress

When I needed to find a new husband, I put on a red, strapless leather dress. "Red is the color to wear to get men," I've been telling my customers for over forty years. The power of red was first revealed to me by Fred Hayman, who owned Giorgio's of Beverly Hills. Fred and his beautiful wife, Gale, were the first to come to Paris to buy my French Couture dress line in 1971. Fred saw my fashion show and was horrified that I only offered "Torrid," my bestselling mummy-draped jersey dress, in black and pastels.

Fred, with the authority of a fashion professor, proclaimed to the staff and the astonished French model, "VICKY, THE FIRST COLOR THAT I SELL A GOWN IN IS BLACK BECAUSE WOMEN LOOK THE SKINNIEST IN BLACK AND THE SECOND COLOR IS RED, SO WOMEN CAN EXCITE MEN."

He was right. When my first husband told me to date, at forty-one, after sleeping in separate bedrooms because I knew he was cheating, I didn't cry or break down but flew to New York, went to a posh party in my red, strapless leather dress with gold strapped heels, and found a gorgeous silver-haired athlete on a couch near the wood burning fireplace. When I put my hand on his muscular knee and squeezed, whoopee, we were at it for several years.

God created a woman in a strapless red dress!

Christie
Brinkley
1986

Red duchess
satin
wrap gown

Vicky Tiel

Worn
with
Billy Joel
and baby
Harpers
Bazaar
Shoot

Ten Life Lessons from a Painful Divorce or Separation

1. Always spin a bad thing in your favor.
2. Learn patience.
3. Be kind to strangers; you never know who's the bum in ripped jeans.
4. Find happiness in everything.
5. Laugh as much as you can. Smile at cute kids, pets, and old folks.
6. Do not try to make anyone love you, only go after the ones who love you.
7. Keep the children out of it.
8. Keep friends and family out of it.
9. Never spy on your ex.
10. Never, never give up on believing that you can...

Jacqueline
Bisset

Backless silk
striped bias
shirtdress

Button-up
front

Cannes Festival
1973

Vicky Tiel

"Every birthday is a gift.
Every day is a gift."

ARETHA FRANKLIN

Meditating to Orgasm Is a Practice of Being in the Moment While Having Sex

Meditation came into my life when I moved with my young, fisherman husband number two to our forty-acre farm in Northwest Florida.

I was cast into the land instead of cast out to sea. I was cast among the long leaf pine trees, with only the noise of wild birds and the rushing river, and there I learned to love the simplicity of being at one with nature. Gone were the fashion parties in all the capital cities and gone was only eating in the Three Michelin Star Parisian restaurants.

It was glorious Nature with a capital N.

Suddenly I was like Scarlett O'Hara at her home, "Tara," but on my own land, my own "Tara," with all its changing critters: foxes, snakes, hawks, panthers, and white-tailed deer replaced my glorious Paris views. Meditating in nature was so easy as there was no noise, only the thoughts in my brain. I decided to learn how to eliminate all my thoughts by letting them just pass through my brain but not staying, thus my body could become one with the surrounding Nature.

I took classes in Third Eye Meditation and then took the meditation lessons into my bedroom, where I learned to close my eyes during sex and look through my third eye, the center of my forehead in front of the pineal gland. I would go deeper into the third eye as it makes a blue tunnel and then I would fast forward into the tunnel with all my lower body sensations going into my consciousness until I came multiple times.

These orgasms are deeper and different than just a feeling in the clitoris. This orgasm is in the entire body, especially in the brain, and in the happiness zone.

I really recommend this to all women. If you achieve this full body orgasm, pass it on and tell your girlfriends. There are many books on Third Eye Meditation. They will thank you.

Whitney
Houston
1998

black
jersey gown

"Avoid fruits and nuts.
You are what you eat."

JIM DAVIS

If God Didn't Make It, Don't Eat It

At seventy-four, I have never dieted, I have never been sick, I have no face lift, no Botox; I am as nature wanted me, two sizes bigger in my chest and waist but the same size as when I was forty in my back, hips, and legs.

I eat healthy and I eat French-style, no prepared food, no packages, and nothing frozen except as a glacé treat, no diet products, no diet drinks, or Sweet and Low. I rarely eat prepared packaged foods except some English or French cookies with my afternoon red fruit teas. I will eat a scoop of great ice cream or a great dessert in a very small portion every day! French people have dessert every day (for happiness) and gain no weight!

Did you know that Americans eat thirty-one percent more packaged food than fresh food? That is way more processed foods than anyone should eat, and it goes against what I've learned from my French lifestyle.

I stopped eating animals that are mothers when I moved to my farm in Florida and saw the dearest cows on my driveway with their precious babies. I do eat healthy fresh fish and the fresh laid eggs from my pet chickens.

My New York-based doctor, Dr. George Y.C. Wong, who is a specialist in Chinese herbal medicine and cancer, told me twenty years ago to eat five to seven fruits and vegetables a day: as many purple, blue, and red foods as possible, then orange foods, then green foods, then yellows and browns and ALMOST NO white food, except maybe one a day. This menu helps prevent cancer as the purple, blue, and red fruits, and red and green vegetables, detox your body, and it keeps me young without doctors. He was right, as I don't even get colds or the flu, even though I travel every two weeks. I did get pneumonia once from trying out a jacuzzi naked at my mountain cabin at midnight in the SNOW.

Don't forget to FEED YOUR BRAIN as it uses twenty to thirty percent of your calories.

If you eat processed food there is no way your brain will last until you are ninety.

DON'T DRINK YOUR CALORIES; EAT GOOD PROTEIN FOR YOUR BRAIN.

Focus on EGGS, FISH, and VEGETABLES—especially PEAS, SPINACH, AVOCADOS, ASPARAGUS, KALE, BROCCOLI, and BRUSSELS SPROUTS.

Vicky's French Grocery Shopping List for Natural Beauty and Natural Aging

My Veggies:

Red peppers	Beets
All beans	Tomatoes (also with just
Spinach	basil and Italian olive oil)
Red or purple tomatoes	Avocados

Asparagus
Broccoli
Kale
Purple lettuce
Sweet Potatoes
Purple or red potatoes
Carrots
Sweet Corn

Red Cabbage
Radish with butter (my only
　　use of butter)
Sun dried tomatoes
French tabouli with mint
Brown rice only with sushi
French celery remoulade
Spices and herbs

My Fruits:

Strawberries in season
Grapefruit
Raspberries
Lemons and limes
Blueberries or blackberries
　　smashed in blueberry
　　yogurt
Red apples

Clementines and oranges
Cranberries
Purple grapes (I freeze them)
Mangoes
Figs and prunes D'Agen,
　　France
Peaches
Pears

I love French cheese.

Blue cheese, goat cheese, Brie, and fresh-sliced Parmesan.

In France, I eat all the cheeses on bread but I do not eat bread in America, except in the morning (because it's different flour). In America I eat my goat cheese on red apples or pears.

I grow fresh basil, parsley, garlic, and mint in pots at my front door, and I buy ginger which I slice to drink in my tea.

I buy fresh baked bread with nuts and berries and French Bonne Maman Blueberry Jam for my toast.

I eat hummus or homemade guacamole with red peppers instead of crackers or corn chips.

NO BUTTER...no margarine, I use fresh Mediterranean olive oil—the Mediterranean diet.

I use fresh coleslaw as a salad dressing, never plain mayo or bottled dressings.

I drink French Carte Noire or Italian Lavazza coffee in a French coffee press with no milk and no sugar.

I drink water but not out of a plastic bottle.

If I have the beginning of a sore throat, I drink lemon tea with fresh honey.

I also drink unsweetened mint tea, red fruit tea, and cranberry juice always in crystal wine glasses to feel special. The crystal glasses make the drinks more interesting and fun; especially since I don't drink alcohol, the glasses make normal drinks feel like a party! If I drank alcohol it would be red wine, but I quit drinking at fifty after crashing five cars in thirty-four years.

Remember ladies, do not have more than five to seven drinks of alcohol a week, depending on your size. HAPPINESS DOES NOT COME IN A BOTTLE of alcohol. After forty, it's best to have three drinks a week, not three bottles.

My dessert is a small scoop of gelato ice cream or yogurt ice cream always covered with blue, black, or red berries and crushed pecans. In France only, I eat crème fraiche with my berries.

I love Italian gelato. The best is Nuchiolo, a chocolate and hazelnut flavor.

At 4:00 pm I have English tea in vintage cups with one English tea biscuit and a nice piece of dark chocolate. I also love milk chocolate from Venezuela.

I eat five times a day with small portions.

Every day I have breakfast at 5:00 am, yogurt at 10:00 am, lunch at 1:00 pm, tea at 4:00 pm, and dinner at 6:30 pm. I go to sleep at 9:30 pm, about three to four hours after my last meal.

I try for six and a half or seven hours of sleep without any prescription meds. I take no meds.

My sport is swimming and every morning I do twenty-one knee bends and touch the floor with my hands. I walk the streets of Paris and NY for hours...ten thousand steps once in a while (with a step-watch).

This au natural lifestyle, pas mal, especially for fifty and over, is a great menu for overweight women, models, actresses, and young people who need to be slim for their work or for their lifestyle, and definitely good for everyone with bad health.

When I go to the movies I will have a bag of popcorn but never a coke.

I'm happy being healthy, and will only go off diet on holidays with my grandkids and in Paris.

When in Paris, I eat French food, as it is not packaged since the French shop daily for their fresh food. When in town, I go to my Paris market near my shop, the Rue de Buci, and I have been going there faithfully each morning for fifty years. On Sunday mornings, you will see me at the Café Buci from 10:00 am until noon, reading the French and British Sunday papers with my Café et Croissant.

I eat by counting my colors. I eat five to seven orange, red, and purple fruits and vegetables, eating 5 times a day.

This is not a special diet, it's how I've lived since I turned fifty.

Breakfast

* French Carte Noire or Italian Lavazzo Espresso; I use a Boudoin coffee press, I drink it black and have 2 cups.
* 2 slices of freshly baked grain bread, no butter ever!
* I prefer whole grain with nuts and berries, toasted with either fresh honey or my homemade peach or pear jam or French Bonne Maman Blueberry Jam covered with real blueberries, raspberries, or blackberries.
* ½ grapefruit, I eat the pulp (pulp helps you live longer, my mother taught me that and she lived to ninety-five and never was sick on this diet) or an orange or two clementines.
* In Paris I have a croissant that I dunk in my cafe creme. You don't gain weight in Paris, you stay the same.
* At breakfast, I usually eat at least two colors.

10:30 am—Snack

* Yogurt with 10 blackberries or raspberries on top, with crushed pecans or walnuts.
* Or a cup of frozen purple grapes, my go-to snack is always in the freezer.
* You can mix your berries in fruit yogurt, smash them, and freeze to replace ice cream.
* With purple and red berries, my snack is also a two-color meal.

12:30 to 1:00 pm—Lunch

* I eat my biggest meal at noon so I have the day to work off the calories.
* I drink iced Moroccan mint tea or red berry tea.

* Italian homemade pasta covered with 1½ cups of whole small tomatoes cut in half that are cooked with asparagus or collard greens, broccoli, or any greens in olive oil (no butter).
* Cracked pepper, oregano, and sliced Parmesan cheese on top. Two colors.
* Or baked wild salmon with red or sweet potatoes and lima beans or asparagus total one color.
* Or I make a salad of the baked salmon, purple lettuce, avocado, almonds, blackberries, with spring coleslaw as my dressing. Total 2 colors.

4:00 pm

* I drink iced tea in tall crystal wine glasses filled with ice and add fresh rosemary, ginger, and lemons (for memory) but no sugar or hot Moroccan mint tea or iced tea with rooibos or Tadin Seven Blossoms.
* In winter, I have sliced ginger tea in antique tea cups.
* And my snack is 2 English tea biscuits or a chocolate square or chocolate covered almonds.
* Tea is usually only one color.

6:00 pm

* I have two cooked or grilled vegetables or a big salad. I love local corn.
* My salad is always different: I fill a big bowl with purple lettuce, tomatoes, avocados, raspberries or any berry, even dried berries, pecans or walnuts, with 6 small chunks of wild caught salmon (baked and covered in maple syrup and brown sugar). Any fruit or vegetable left in the refrigerator, I chop it up.

* My salad dressing is always spring coleslaw. I put a half cup in and toss.
* Sometimes I'll have sliced cold beets with chèvre goat cheese and topped with green onions with iced unsweetened mint tea with lemon.
* After dinner I eat a bunch of frozen purple grapes.
* Dessert is a few dark-chocolate-covered almonds.
* Dinner is usually two (often more) colors.

This diet prevents cancer and any other disease.

It deoxidizes the body. It gives you endless energy.

If I'm tired and need a sugar boost, I'll pop an almond covered in dark chocolate, not a pill or white sugar.

I am seventy-five, have never been sick, and work all day, sleep six and a half hours at night and fly every ten days or so. I don't drink or do drugs, I only take Vitamin D.

I see a doctor once a year, Dr. Vishwanath (from India) in Florala, Alabama, and he gets me as I like natural medicine.

I love timeless fashion!

*"I drink to make other people
more interesting."*

ERNEST HEMINGWAY

You Are What You Drink

You are what you drink after forty (since you are eighty percent liquid).

After years of study on drinking I came up with this perfectly "healthy drinks" diet.

Men and women do take note:

Every day for breakfast I drink French coffee Carte Noir or Italian Lavazzo espresso with no milk or sugar, except when in Paris, where I have a large cafe crème but with no sugar. I carry my French coffee in my bags and a French press so I just need boiled water.

With all my meals, I drink iced herbal Moroccan mint tea with three lemon slices, no sugar or water.

Every afternoon I have Moroccan mint or a ginger tea with lemon, no sugar, in vintage teacups. (My client, Baronne Aimee de Herron, lived to 103 on daily ginger tea.)

At parties when others drink alcohol, I drink Perrier in a champagne glass.

If I feel a cold coming on, I drink chamomile or ginger tea with lemon and honey.

I drink rosemary and ginger and lemon herb tea for memory.

I try to have four to five glasses of water a day.

At the oceanside restaurants, I'll have a cocktail of a frozen, non-alcoholic piña colada.

Even though I stopped drinking alcohol twenty-four years ago, I am still able to party and socialize with others who drink and not have any desires to return to a life of Dom Pérignon champagne and Grand Cru French (only) wines, because I feel better sober when I'm older.

I've stayed with one husband, so I can't get high and get crazy.

And, most of all, after totaling five cars when I did drink, I haven't totaled one since.

In hot summer months, I'll drink POM Wonderful pomegranate drink in crystal wine glasses.

It is wonderful and produced by my Beverly Hills dress client, Lynda Resnick.

If I were to drink alcohol it would be a healthy glass of red wine with dinner, not white, as the French claim drinking white wine made the Germans invade them.

I have discovered that my clients who drink any type of soda pop (especially diet soda) have shorter lives and fatter stomachs than women who follow my drinking diet. I recognize the diet drinks in their body fat—it's puckered.

Also, as our bodies are eighty percent liquid, you are what you drink.

Drink smart and learn to love what's good for you.

If I live to be ninety, I'll have a glass of Dom Pérignon on Saturday night instead of old folks' meds.

Christmas 2017. View from my Paris home.

"Food is like sex:
When you abstain, even the worst
stuff begins to look good."

BETH McCOLLISTER

My Sunday Special Diet

Breakfast never changes, nor does my coffee mug. I have the same mug I bought in Switzerland with Elizabeth Taylor and her daughter Liza; we all still use the same dishes that are hand painted Swiss mountain scenes.

10:30am snack is two of my chicken's fresh eggs made into a vegetable omelette.

With a cooked base of thirty small tomatoes cut in half, in olive oil, add greens, and pour over the whipped-up eggs.

I use Dijon mustard, not ketchup, with my eggs.

I drink iced tea all day, with lemons and limes.

Lunch is grilled fish—either salmon, tuna, bass, or grouper—with baked red sweet potatoes and a chopped avocado salad with spring slaw.

4:00pm tea is hot tea in my English cups.

My berry or apple pie with yogurt ice cream: I eat a small amount of pie with lots of fruit and a spoonful of yogurt ice cream. In Florida, I love key lime pie.

Sometimes, I'll just have yogurt ice cream covered in mixed berries or a huge snack of dried figs and English biscuits.

For 6:00pm dinner I make a salad with the fish from lunch and add nuts, berries, and coleslaw dressing, followed by a great dessert of a blueberry pie à la mode.

1968, Mia and I in the shop wearing sexy wool jersey jumpsuits, the first in Paris. They were created in 1964 for What's New Pussycat?

"To me, beauty is about being comfortable in your own skin. It's about knowing and accepting who you are."

ELLEN DEGENERES

Yes or No to Plastic Surgery

It's me or it's not me.

Do I or do I not redo my face? Who am I?

Is it truly powerful to not grow old as you were meant to?

Coco Chanel, Elizabeth Arden, and Helena Rubinstein all died naturally. None of them altered their faces. Today, Angela Merkel, the most powerful woman in the world, is as she was made. Did she feel Botox was not a power move?

I feel that as long as you are recognizable, it's okay, but to alter yourself into a cartoon of yourself is a choice and to me it's a choice of Visible Insecurity.

To me a huge smile is a sign of youth.

To me a vital body is a sign of youth.

I recommend instead buying a gym membership or a pool for the price of a facelift and years of Botox.

I look in the mirror and I see ME, my pal, Miss Vicky.

We've gone a long way, we've had too much fun.

Some questions to ask yourself:

* Do you need a wrinkle-free face for work, especially if you are in show biz or on TV?
* Does your man want it?
* Are you afraid of losing him, even though he has dark circles under his eyes and a face full of wrinkles?
* Will you be a different person to him?
* Would you really want to change your man's face?
* Would you love him with a shiny wrinkle-free face?

Maybe you don't change yourself or your man.

Maybe you correct your extra twenty pounds first, as overweight people tend to die first.

Maybe before you focus on the outer you, you focus on the inner you.

Joanna
Shimpkus /
later
Mme
Sidney
Poitier
1967

blue crepe
wrap dress
worn during
"BOOM"

Vicky
Tiel

Quiet the voice inside you,
the voice that never shuts up,
when you walk, when you sleep,
even when you wake up, quiet this
voice through self-realization,
finding out who you are.

MICHAEL A. SINGER, *THE UNTETHERED SOUL*

So Long, Peaches

It's hard to get over being the most drooled over woman in the room. I was asked in the '60s, "Aren't you afraid to walk on the streets in public in those see-thru lace mini dresses without underwear?" and I replied, "Nobody raped Marilyn Monroe walking down the street. They freeze under her power."

My twenties were all about getting my picture taken, walking into a party in a dress nobody had ever seen before, like a purple crochet jumpsuit with orange eyes on the breast and red lips on the crotch, a design from my "Think Dirty Paris" collection of 1969.

I eventually became more interested in selling my fashions in my thirties and giving power from fashion to others, and so, I decided to sell fashions worldwide and quit the movies, as Edith Head said I couldn't do both film costumes and retail. Choosing to put the power of seduction in my clothes, I could help women everywhere to seduce men.

My forties were about finding a faithful second husband, someone who really was crazy about just me.

My fifties and sixties were about finding out who I really was and writing about this discovery.

Vicky as Peaches LaTour

Walking Wuffles
in Greenwich Village
1963

bikini made of
fresh leaves

VickyTiel

"I feel happy and secure when
I'm on my bed with a good book...
I forget everything which is
terrible in our world."

FRANÇOISE HARDY

The Power of Philosophy

Living in France for most of my life and bringing up two French children, I learned about the power that philosophy has over one's life. In fact, if you asked what profession makes a man hot in France, I would put philosophy right after being a chef.

My son Rex was best friends in school with Raphaël Enthoven, now a philosopher, who fathered the model Carla Bruni's son. Carla later married the much older President, Nicolas Sarkozy, after she also had an affair with Raphaël's father's best friend, France's leading philosopher, Bernard-Henri Lévy, who is a regular on French TV and also the husband of French movie star, Arielle Dombasle. Bernard-Henri Lévy is also the lover of millionaire artist, Daphne Guinness. Bernard-Henri Lévy: a man so hot that two famous French beauties have accepted to publicly share him. And he's a philosopher.

While living in France, I discovered my favorite philosopher, Joseph Campbell, in the Bill Moyers documentary "The Power of Myth." More people know Joseph Campbell in France than America, his country of birth. Campbell, a professor at Sarah Lawrence for thirty-eight years, explains that all human life has a lesson to be learned before death, and that each individual is capable of this lesson at a given point of their life.

Campbell believed in Kundalini Yoga. The Indian explanation of Kundalini Yoga is that the three chakras above the neck differentiate us from animals, who only share the four lower chakras (sexual, anger, hunger, urges), but have no higher consciousness. The chakras above the neck (throat chakra, third eye chakra, crown chakra) can be developed in each human at a different time in life through enlightened experiences. Campbell called these Myths, and each Myth experience transformed our consciousness until our death.

I actually had my personal, life-transforming experience in Egypt, seated inside the great Pyramid at Giza in the King's Chamber when I felt my choice of my second husband was a mistake and someone else was out there for me. I called my banker fiancée as soon as I left the Pyramid on my camel, only to find that he had taken the opportunity of my very distant desert holiday with my two sons to cheat on me at the Hilton Head golf club with his partner's mistress.

Egypt—the sand, the antiquities, the thousands of years of culture—cleared my mind and the universe was telling me to change directions. I was about to make a major life mistake. I also found an ancient blue perfume bottle in a Giza desert shop and decided I would make my own perfumes in the same antique blue bottle as soon as I returned to Paris. The perfume business has since enriched my life and allows me to never retire.

Of course, I was ready for the transformations, as I had read Joseph Campbell. My marriage was over, my next man was over. Meditating in the Great Pyramid gave me a direct message from God: Your life decisions are wrong, Vicky. "Move on," I was told from heaven, and happily I did.

Trippy and I on the farm in Florida.

"There is no path to happiness.
Happiness is the path."

GUATAMA BUDDHA

The Art of Happiness

Own your own business. Better yet, if you can, do not involve your father, your mother, your best friend—and especially not your husband—as he can threaten you, fire you, or even replace you with another woman. A husband backer is a risk I've seen backfire once too often. A bank is better. The Art of Happiness is the Art of Independence: only be responsible for yourself. (Unless you are SURE to have the world's best partner.) I did with my best friend, and she still left me to follow her dream and become a sculptress.

There are two types of people in general: Those Fearless and Those Fearful. You know who you are. If you are fearless, you find out what talent you have, what you are good at, what makes you happy, and DO IT! Get a business plan, find money, and build your business.

If you are fearful, forget about it and get a job, find a good boss, and don't look back. Enjoy the life of semi-security and use your intuition to know who in the company is climbing up the ladder and hitch your wagon to them. Team players and company owners have different sets of skills and need each other.

I remember once in my Paris atelier having words with Nicole, the chef d'atelier of the Couture boutique, for having left early before a bride's dress was finished. Instead of saying a "oui, madame," Nicole grabbed the scissors and ran after me screaming, "I'm not you, I don't own anything." At that moment I realized we are all created differently: workaholics, perfectionists, and everybody else.

I recently spoke about fashion at an event in New York with fashion designers Zandra Rhodes and Anna Sui. There we were, three survivors of our own fashion houses: one French, one Brit, and one American, all women owners. We met for lunch in mid Manhattan. Fashion is the only industry that requires four collections a year, four possibilities of failure every year. You and your ego are put through the test. Will somebody buy my work? If you fail twice, you are history.

None of us three were worse for wear. We actually thrived on the challenge and looked as delicious as the food, considering our total age was about 200.

Much like myself after a forty-year career, Zandra did something else; she opened her own museum in London dedicated to fashion and textile. She had spent her life in fashion, as her mother had been a fitter at Worth in Paris, and Zandra went into owning her own design company in her twenties in London, by designing her own fabrics and sewing her first dresses in her unique prints.

Anna Sui proved the challenges and rewards of owning your own company—as you are the artist, agent, manager, and publicist. You often trade off being the top of your field for being the top of your own little world. Anna Sui's little world grew into a huge multi-million-dollar empire.

However, if you are Martha Stewart, who left a fifteen-year career on Wall Street to cater parties in her posh Westport, Connecticut suburb, you can have it all. We all know today that she is fearless. She ventured into Manhattan for her first job and catered my opening party in Bergdorf Goodman. It was 1981 and she served sushi herself, passing the tray to the richest women in America. Martha brought taste and the arts into the modern American home, and in her first video she wore my beaded black gown, the same beaded gown worn in white by Elizabeth Taylor after her eighth wedding. The perfect power dress for the fearless female. Martha knew where she was going.

There is the rare exception to the rule about working with your man. The husband and wife team of Amy Zerner and Monte Farber who left their jobs as a fine artist and a musician, respectively, to write over forty bestselling oracles on spirituality, all illustrated by Amy. They became a mom-and-pop conglomerate. They have no children, their togetherness knows no end, as their team and their work *is* their baby. Amy added fashion and jewelry and they opened a store in the Hamptons and sold next to me at Bergdorf Goodman. Amy told me she has lived out Joseph Campbell's mantra, "Follow Your Bliss." I have never met another couple so unique, but they prove it's possible, and they are both artists.

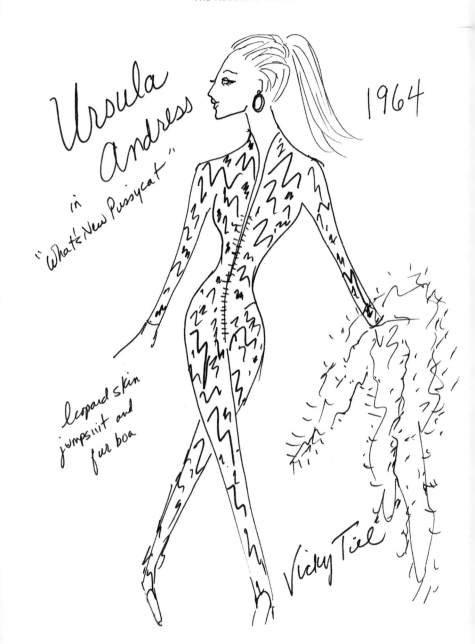

Ursula Andress in "What's New Pussycat"

1964

leopard skin jumpsuit and fur boa

Vicky Tiel

Talent is God given. Be humble.
Fame is man-given. Be grateful.
Conceit is self-given. Be careful.

JOHN WOODEN

The World is Divided into Two Groups: Artists and Everyone Else

I told my friends this in the early '60s. Sometimes my non-artist friends wanted to hit me on the head—I could see it in their eyes. Artists see the world in different colors. Art becomes our God and achieving our goals can become more important than food, family, or friends.

Times have changed. Today the world is one; everything has changed as Earth is a smaller planet in this ever-expanding universe and art and artists are spreading everywhere, joining forces as fast as the freedom demonstrators, in this ever-expanding, internet-ruled world.

Have courage, artists, and assume the world is waiting for you. We did. I created the mini skirt with my partner Mia Fonssagrives in fashion school in New York and had the courage to cross the Atlantic on a boat with eighteen suitcases and my dog, Wuffles, to go to Paris in May 1964. Without the internet, just newspaper and magazine coverage, we were showing the mini on the Johnny Carson Show by December 1964. This is the principle for success for artists: courage!

Don't listen to the naysayers. Do your thing, follow your dreams, create the new invention in your garage, like Steve Jobs, sew the new wrap skirt on your machine, like Mia, make the best book on entertaining, like Martha. Why not? Fear of failure? We did it.

Today, with the internet, it's so easy to create a new design and sell it without a middleman. There are websites galore, selling every possible design from clothes to furniture. Today there are people who can't design looking for products to sell, or products to promote. That person is closer to twenty than sixty.

Artists who are older like myself are also looking for the next, next thing. I wanted to stop selling expensive French Couture and turned to selling my products on HSN TV and online. On TV, I sold a wrap dress printed in fourteen colors, which were applied individually in France in the '60s. Today with the photocopy prints, the wrap dress copy costs less to make than it did back in 1969.

The internet also changed how I could teach fashion, by creating a video for The University of Fashion. I no longer had to visit schools to pass on my expertise.

Now a young girl in Namibia, Africa, can start her own fashion house.

Brooke
Shields

1985

atchdam
silk suit
with
pearls

covered
buttons
down front

bustle back skirt

Vicky Tiel

"Act as if what you do makes a difference. It does."

WILLIAM JAMES

Children are Changing the World

I call this new generation the Selfie Generation. My generation, the '60s Revolutionary Generation, has returned in spirit today with a new name, the Selfie Generation. The Selfie has the power, the ambition, and the tools to radically change the world. In spite of their name, they are not about ME for themselves—they are ready to send themselves into the world.

My '60s generation was all about "making love not war," loving the Beatles and the Stones, creating a fashion and a sexual revolution, demanding the end of racial and religious judgement, and conceiving the idea that humans can gather and march for a belief and not get shot. Since my generation, we have not had a generation that stood out and made a difference until now.

Sadly, the children of my generation were determined to be the opposite of their crazy parents and became the ME-ME entitlement generation, living for happiness, their own personal happiness, with their love of craft beer, healthy cooking, decorating, yoga, massages, skin care, zombies, and kickboxing.

Their babies, now teens, are very different, as the Selfie has taken their photo out into the whole world. The Selfie is concerned about the planet and what is left for them. Many teens tell me they are getting ready to leave for other planets. They are already using robots at home and using iPhones to text everywhere all the time, and they are afraid of nothing. They will discover the entree into the other dimensions. The galaxy awaits.

The Selfie generation is also generous. For the first time in history DoSomething.org reports the list of the most generous celebrities are under thirty years old. The chart is topped by Taylor Swift, teenage boy band One Direction, and wild girl Miley Cyrus.

Here are a few of the young, female leaders of today who are changing the world:

Politics

At fourteen, Malala Yousafzai stood up for female education and was shot, but fought back and lived to become a political force in Pakistan. Will she lead Middle Eastern woman to equality?

Art and Fashion

At twenty-one, Miley Cyrus turned heads with her music video "Wrecking Ball," and her fashion-as-wearable-art has opened up the world to a new look in feminine fashion. If I were twenty, I would dress like Miley. I even bought her entire Walmart collection, which she designed at sixteen.

Music

At sixteen, Lorde wrote "Royals" and the world listened to her poetry. She went to the top of the charts with her digitally-released first album, and she's from New Zealand.

Cinema

Jennifer Lawrence won the Oscar at twenty-two and she brings back memories of our '60s heroine, Audrey Hepburn, who won her first Oscar at twenty-three. At twenty, Adele Exarchopoulos won the César at the Cannes Film Festival with "Blue is the Warmest Color," my favorite film of 2013. She stole the movie, crying at least ten times, and she even cried with snot, which is nearly impossible. (I did costumes on sixteen movies and I know.)

With my grandchildren.

"Fashion is not for sissies."

MICHAEL KORS

The History of Paris Ready-to-Wear

It's a little-known fact today but Paris ready-to-wear, as we know it today, was started in the late '50s by a beautiful brunette, a Balenciaga model named Emmanuelle Khanh.

I had the pleasure to dine with Emmanuelle a few years back in her two-level artist studio in Montparnasse. We discussed the coming debut of the twice-yearly circus, known today as Paris Fashion Week. Emmanuelle said to me, "Fashion is no longer prêt-à-porter, but prêt-à-montrer." (It's all show.)

In 1957, Emmanuelle and Christiane Bailly met as they modeled in the top couture houses. Wanting to outdo the other models, Emmanuelle had a dressmaker create a low-cut, cotton culottes dress that caused a stir on the Faubourg Saint-Honoré. With the backing of Boussac, the French cotton king, Emmanuelle and Christiane presented their first collection in 1959. They showed modern sportswear, culottes, long droopy collars on tops, shorter bias skirts, and, by using menswear fabric such as Harris Tweed, they made shorter fitted dresses, as the dresses before had been boxy or long. This new soft, clingy, easy-to-sew fashion became a big hit among post-war Parisiennes.

Elle magazine was the first news, fashion, and lifestyle magazine in France for the young, hip generation. Started by Helene Lazareff, the wife of newspaper owner of *France-Soir*, *Elle* showed Emmanuelle's first collection and Michèle Rosier, the daughter of Helene Lazareff, also got into the act and produced coats in black vinyl, that preceded today's puffy coat. These styles were called prêt-à-porter (ready to wear).

Until the late '50s, clothes in France were produced by small companies for the department stores Prisunic and Galeries Lafayette without designers, often produced in factories near Lyon where the fabric was made—but these garments were not fashion, just clothes.

Fashion was seen only in the twice-yearly Haute Couture presentations in the designer's small showrooms. Fashion was controlled by twenty Couture houses, and women sewed at home or used a dressmaker to make their clothing.

When I arrived in Paris in 1964, we joined these three women and Mia and I were called the YE-YE girls. We actually went on a design interview at Royaume and lost the job to a young German, Karl Lagerfeld. It was his first label. Then, Kenzo arrived from Japan, and Sonia Rykiel became a brand, after she left her job designing sweaters for her husband's store, Laura. Slowly, a small group of ready-to-wear designers was formed and specialty shops such as MADD and Dorothée Bis featured our designs. We were all signed in America by Carl Rosen (the father of the owner of Theory, Inc.) and the worldwide youth fashion began.

The first Paris ready-to-wear shows were silent somber affairs in art galleries, restaurants, and clubs. It would slowly become show biz when my press pal, Yanou Collart, surprised Paris with live music in my first solo fashion show in the Salle Wagram, where Marlon Brando comically danced the Tango in his film, *The Last Tango in Paris*. We served butter on every table and Paris loosened up.

Emmanuelle Khanh ruled Paris socially in the '70s and '80s. Her oversized white eyeglasses made her a fortune. She and her husband, Quasar Khanh, bought a 1930s pink marble mansion belonging to a prince in a posh suburb west of Paris. On Saturday night, their home was the center of the swinging Paris fashion scene, as you had to arrive in a fabulous car wearing antique ball gowns and major jewels. I actually wore a silver lamé gown and a feathered headdress and will never forget the night, in our navy Maserati convertible, as we crossed the Seine with all the lights at the Place de la Concorde and drove on to her hillside palace. I was right in a movie.

With Emmanuelle Khanh

"When death comes to you,
may it find you alive."

AFRICAN SAYING

If You Love YSL, Read This Story

t's 2007 and YSL, Pierre Berge, Sonia Rykiel, Emmanuelle Khanh, and myself—now all old and wrinkled and not so fabulous anymore—are all seated par hasard on the same banquette in Paris. We were all five, by accident, eating at the Brasserie Lipp. It's impossible but true. I thought I'd seen it all in my fifty years in Paris fashion but this night was the highlight for me. In French it's called *Le dénouement*. This evening proves that success and happiness is not all about money.

Here's what happened. In early Fall 2007, Emmanuelle called me at my Paris shop at 21 Rue Bonaparte (like my perfume), to tell me she was retiring from fashion and wanted to celebrate with me. Could I meet her for a "verre" at the Cafe Flore and afterwards dinner at Brasserie Lipp? I happily replied YES.

At the Flore, she told me (as she's now divorced), that she was leaving fashion because the big corporations were taking over all the fashion brands, and the industry was destroyed because they had thrown out the real designers and only wanted to sell accessories. We stared at Dior as we crossed the street. There were no clothes in the windows, only handbags and shoes and perfume. Fashion clothing was unsalable; it was only an overblown show for the press for publicity to create a brand.

After drinks, we walked into the Brasserie Lipp where we were seated on the far-wall red banquette, the top spot where Mr. Caze puts only the most famous celebrities and the in-favor politicians.

We were early and were placed at the center of the red leather banquette. Emmanuelle ordered more champagne, I ordered lemonade, and we discussed the last year's fashion insanity, and we roared with laughter while a very somber Sonia Rykiel walked in with her elderly boyfriend; they were placed next to us on the banquette. "Bonjours" were padded around with kisses on both cheeks and then more somber silence. Minutes later, Yves Saint Laurent and Pierre Berge walked in and were placed next to Sonia and her boyfriend. All par hasard. A deathly silence from YSL and Berger, not even a "bonjour," and they didn't even talk to each other. Not a word.

Today, I understand the deathly silence from Sonia. She had just learned she had Parkinson's and would soon die. That night ten years ago, she was so sad and miserable as she learned she would be unable to hide her disease. Yves Saint Laurent was also months away from dying. They were four souls waiting for an execution. I was later told by a fabric house that we both shared, that Yves, at the end of his career, drank an entire bottle of scotch while buying fabric. That's only two to three hours to drink an entire bottle. Today I have over my desk a photo of Yves and his dog, Moujik, leaving work for the last time on Ave George V in 2002. His head was down. It reminds me that I want to work until I die, like Coco. Happily, I drank no more.

I was saddened to see the miserable designers next to me. We never said another word to them, nor they to us. However, nothing could stop Emmanuelle and myself from having a wonderful evening of memories, laughing until we cried, even more so with the miserable billionaires next to us. Sadly, Emmanuelle died just as I was writing my book. She had cancer, but she never told me or anyone.

Artists will understand this story. Fame and money do not buy happiness. Van Gogh, Rothko, L'Wren Scott, Alexander McQueen, Kate Spade, and Anthony Bourdain all killed themselves, in spite of having enormous talent and lives other artists could only dream of. Artists understand that they must tolerate suffering in order to create and few artists are able to leave their craft and walk away. Suffering is not necessary to create. Happiness is another Art. I work at Happiness.

Gayle King

"I am a woman of the most
extraordinary vitality.
I have never been bored
for a second.
I have never been envious of
anyone or anything, and now I have
achieved a certain tranquility."

MADELEINE VIONNET

How the World Has Changed: It is Now One

Today, with the internet, everything is known. If Paris has a new coral jean with a ripped hem, it is already available half price in Bloomingdale's, and a week later it's just twenty-nine dollars at Target. Even the children's department will have coral jeans for girls and boys in a month. There is now world-wide fashion. Forget copyright laws and exclusivity, world-wide fashion is the new democracy. Watch the airports: seven out of ten women are wearing black stretch pants and various tops. I call this the WORLD UNIFORM. I decided to join the world.

I was the first French Couture designer to sell products on TV. I decided to give the American public an Elizabeth Taylor caftan, the Liza, and one dress that sold for 8,790 dollars at Christie's was copied for TV for 129 dollars.

For decades I had been asked to manufacture less expensive clothing in China. Once, in the late 1990s, I was asked by the charming Oleg Cassini (then eighty-five) to meet him for drinks at the St. Regis Bar. He asked me to make clothes in China with Hero Industries. He also asked if I would sleep with him at his townhouse. I answered that the production quality was not up to my standards and that I had a forty-year-old husband and would not consider breaking my marriage vows. Oleg was not used to being turned down either.

I was ready now (at least for China).

I was also ready for television. At twenty-one, I was on Johnny Carson, holding my Yorkie and smoking a cigarette, wearing a French mini that I would sell to American stores. Today, I will sell clothing and perfumes on TV and begin again.

NEW WORLD FASHION

STRETCH PANTS + TOPS

ALL AGES

23 yrs old

50 yrs old

70 yrs old

14 yrs old

PANTS are Hollywood Hip by Vicky Tiel

35 yrs old

"If they don't copy you,
you're no good."

IRVING PENN

The Wrap Dress

Fashion historians take note: The mystery of who invented or created the wrap dress is forever solved!

You might ask, "Does it matter in the scheme of things?" Well, Irving Penn also said, "You know you're good when they take your ideas," and Louis Féraud added, "Ideas are in the air for plucking."

Yes, it matters to me, and should to other Fashionistas with their own creations. Today the truth can be fact checked and the publisher of my first book, St. Martin's Press, checked, as did HSN, before they announced on air that VICKY TIEL (with Mia) created the wrap, the mini, and hot pants.

My very first wrap (with fitted waist, long set-in sleeves, and draped skirt) was in the movie *Candy* in 1968, in a scene with Ringo Starr and the actress Ewa Aulin. The wrap dress was in a *Redbook* magazine in 1968 and in Bloomingdale's windows in 1968.

Today, there are still designers who can do it all, but many are celebrity designers who hire someone like myself, who draws, sews, drapes, fits, and sells. Almost no designers sell.

But Coco taught me to measure, fit, and sell, and be real. Be the dressmaker. God bless my mentor, Coco Chanel.

The point is, I did not kill myself or become a drug addict when DVF made the wrap into a household word, and made millions of them, not thousands. She made it famous.

I did not fall apart at all. I moved on to make the only dress selling at Neiman Marcus for thirty-two straight years. I did other things and, in time, I did get credit for the wrap when I did TV. I did no suing or fighting or anything. I moved on and was rewarded as the longest lasting female fashion designer in France. Now it's been fifty-three years and I'm still working.

Remember, if you accept the bad thing, it often leads to the good thing; it leads to where you are meant to go.

Grandma
and
Lucie Belle
in WRap
dresses.

"Clothes aren't going to
change the world.
The women who wear them will."

ANNE KLEIN

Online Shopping

The Fashion World Revolution began in 1994 with online shopping. Fashion today, and fashion as we knew it, will never be the same again. Brick-and-mortar stores in middle America are closing faster than skirt lengths can change. (If you can still sell a skirt!)

The *Kansas City Business Journal* wrote in May 2017 that all six of the local Gordmans stores were closing; that many of JC Penney's 140 stores would be closing in Kansas City; and that in middle America, Payless shoe store would close 1000 stores, Macy's would close 100 stores, and the local Christian-themed retailer would close all of its stores.

Ladies, go to your closet and pull out twenty things you have not worn for the last two years, and put them on a rack. Photograph them and sell them online at Poshmark, Tradesy, thredUP, and Le Tote, and with that money you can shop for this year. This year you will go in person to a mall or a free-standing store about seventy-five percent less time then you would have five years ago.

Online today, the same shopping site, Polyvore, has a pre-worn couture dress of mine for 1,985 dollars and an

HSN dress of mine for forty-eight dollars. There are sites for people to sell clothes out of their closet and the same sites for people to shop at well-known stores. It's one easy, breezy internet world. There are online sites to rent party clothes for a night, and sites to rent day-wear clothes for a month. Buying clothes in stores is now mainly for the over fifty-five, who love to touch what they buy as they are used to the feeling. Young women are not. (They would rather go kickboxing, or march in a band.)

In my life as a fashion designer for over fifty years, I produced 20,000 couture and 20,000 ready-to-wear pieces, half of which will be sold and resold at lower prices than brick-and-mortar stores. There is no need for me to produce more product, except that I love to work.

Speaking of the future, my eyes really opened to the new fashion world when I began 2017 with a ladies lunch on January 2 in the St. Pete home of Noka Posh designer, Tatjana, and her 8-year-old son, Novak. Tatjana and Novak greeted me at the door with Meccano, his robot and his robot's pet U2. Novak built Meccano himself, his BFF who follows his master around the house, talking and giving and taking instructions. Star Wars is here. The future is here and we had better embrace it as Novak and his generation will soon rule the world. Who knows where artificial intelligence will take us. Robots are already introduced in the workplace, restaurants, and some homes.

The tech generation of Novak will be going to other planets and taking their robot companions with them, as we took our teddy bears to summer camp. Our great grandchildren will be living on other planets in outer space, learning how to time travel through portals. CERN in Switzerland just announced we have eleven dimensions on Earth alone.

Many of our offspring will leave Planet Earth forever with fond memories, but with the tech knowledge we have yet no clue about today. Our grandchildren will be learning more about death and reincarnation, thoughts we have no clear idea about yet, thoughts of how life works and who and what we really are.

As for fashion, clothing will one day be "sprayed on our bodies" by some tech machine as per our desire and our circumstance, and this new fashion process will make the inventor as rich as the inventor of the computer.

We will have dressing rooms with avatars that have our bodies and faces on screens to help us select styles and machines that spray on bottoms and tops, maybe even with individualized outerwear, so we can still have our own identity as to our origins with some creativity in color and pattern. The clothes will be of a spray-on fiber that will work with the detective screens that will be everywhere, especially in all doorways, to see through our clothes to be sure we have no weapons.

Our fashion clothes of today and yesteryear will be in internet museums, and in historical archives, in modern buildings, in towers that humans can view on their travels in automated cars and in trains in the sky.

My first husband, Ron Berkeley, once told me, "If the film writers put it in the movies, it will exist for mankind in fifty years." Star Wars is near.

Speaking of the future, fashion in 2018 has already changed dramatically from recent years. In every city (except the Middle East), women today from five to eighty-five have a world uniform: black tight stretch pants and a soft top. In the warm climates, it's just a T-shirt top; in colder climates, it's a T-shirt top with a black puffy coat, called a puffer.

I watch women in the international airports, in Paris, London, New York, where all planes converge. It's my job. If you sit at the exit café for an hour or two and watch the clothes come off the international airplanes, you can see the world uniform that is now for real. One woman out of 100 wears a dress or skirt. Only one woman out of ten is NOT wearing the world uniform.

Never before in fashion history has a world uniform been worn on Earth (except for the caveman in the real fur look) and someday soon the Middle Eastern women will revolt and wear the world uniform too.

What has this done for fashion designers, like myself, that produce material clothing? We are selling our names as brands for accessories, beauty, home, and exercise products. And if you haven't got a name that is a brand by now, you are left sewing wedding dresses, the one fashion product left today that women want to buy that is NOT PREWORN. Designers can also do costumes for the theater, Vegas-style shows, ballet, and opera.

What will become of the strip malls? What will we do with the time we spent shopping? I predict the malls will become wellness centers, beauty spas, yoga and meditation centers, even judo and kickboxing studios, and they will become medical home centers where we learn to eat healthier, and get our fat eliminated, so we look perfect in our sprayed-on clothes. They will become medical offices. Also, in the south—especially in the south—they will be become religious centers, religious schools, practical extensions of "churches" where there were malls.

Food and pharmaceuticals will be delivered to our homes by electric cars and low-flying drones. Sports centers will grow as the beautiful body will be worshipped. Americans will learn to play rugby and the Brits will play basketball. Art will be available to all and furniture will evolve, traded in like our dresses. Artists, musicians, writers, and movie stars will be bigger and better than ever as humans adore to worship other humans, and animals will be protected from cruelty as fake fur and fake suede will be sprayed on. If I eat my fruits and vegetables, maybe I can live to 110. Hopefully, I can live to see the Brave New World.

I can't wait!

Sarah
Jessica
Parker

"My mother was right:
When you've got nothing left,
all you can do is get into
silk underwear and start
reading Proust."

JANE BIRKIN

Chickens and Couture

I spent forty years, from 1964 to 2004, going to balls in Paris, New York, London, Palm Beach, Vienna, and Budapest. I even went to The Zoo Ball in New Orleans. My life was all about balls, as I made the gowns in Paris for the hostesses of the balls.

In 1986, I won an award as one of the Ten Best Dressed Women of the Year in Paris, along with Princess Soraya and Daisy, the head of her court, Gina Lollobrigida, and Lauren Hutton (one of my ex-husband's "flirts").

Twenty years later, with my younger husband number two, I currently wear a vintage white organdy and lace twenties dress while working in my chicken house with my white baby bantam chickens. I dress like Marie Antoinette who played at Versailles on her farm, with my straw hats from Chanel in the twenties and my vintage straw baskets dolled up with velvet ribbons for feeding greens to the chickens.

My chicks all love it when I arrive dolled up in their 1000 square foot chicken house with a white picket fence on the inside walls and baby blue paint for the ceiling/sky.

They yell "Cock-a-Doodle-Do" to their mom. How do I do both Couture and Chickens?

I do what makes me happy! I dressed Jill Biden for the Presidential Inauguration, and dressed Ivana and Melania Trump in pink to match Donald's ties.

I dress whomever wants to buy my gowns, so I can now dress up for my chickens.

Life doesn't have to be just one thing.

Jane Birkin

Vicky Tiel

lime green jersey peasant gown with ruffle around short sides tie belt

worn with her signature basket

1970's

I'm going to retire
and live off my savings.
What I'll do the second day,
I have no idea.

UNKNOWN

Life, Part Two

For most people today, a retirement job is now necessary, as we will never have enough money from our savings to enjoy a great end of life unless we are in the one percent.

Also, a retirement job is an opportunity to live out our personal dreams. After living for sixty-five years, we all know what we love and don't love and we can now only do what we love.

If you live in the country:

* Open a jam business from your peach or pear trees with your own logo.
* Be a resident assistant and work with the sick or the elderly, who are now a huge part of the population.
* Help in an animal shelter or in a zoo.
* Be a librarian or a personal assistant.

If you live in the suburbs:

* Throw make-up parties in your home.
* Work in a yoga shop.
* Work in a country club.

* Become a bookkeeper or restaurant hostess.
* Do consulting on your own expertise.

If you live in the city:

* Work in retail.
* Become a dressmaker.
* Work at a toy store.
* Open a bakery store with your daughter.
* Be a consultant or a mentor.
* Open a pet-sitting business and hire pet walkers.
* Or, like myself, write a book.

Women who have worked until their death have lived ten to twenty years longer than women who retire and do nothing.

Grandma Moses only started to paint oils at seventy-eight. She became one of America's most beloved women. She died at 101 after painting 1,500 oils and was honored at the White House by President Harry Truman.

Pick out what you love at fifty and start buying your paints, become a sculptress, a pottery maker, and get ready for your Life Part Two Job.

Top: *My wedding to Ron Berkeley in 1971 at the Chelsea Town Hall in London with a Rolls Royce, a loan from Richard Burton and Elizabeth Taylor.* Bottom: *My wedding to Mike Hamilton in 1996 on the riverbank of our Florida farm. I wore Ivana Trump's returned wedding suit.*

"The ones that love us
never really leave us."

HARRY POTTER

Sassy

My beloved dog Sassy, a beautiful German Shepherd "police dog," died suddenly of cancer. She was perfect, she was happy, and at ten years old, she was chasing bright colored tennis balls and scaring chickens when I left her on the farm to go to work on TV. I never imagined those were my last perfect moments with a creature who had stood by me through the death of my dad and the death of my mom (both at once). Both my parents had lived on our Florida farm until their late nineties. The house was so quiet; the precious old folks were gone. Now my beloved Sassy was gone too.

After my parents' death, my husband's dad began to die. It was all too much for my husband Mike—he left me on our farm without any notice! Mike moved to south Florida to "work!"

I now had the farm to myself. Mike was now living in St. Pete, near HSN. He left the farm to work as a fish cutter and a chef at the world-famous beach. He was bored on the farm, he said, as he drove off one day. It was complicated, but we are complicated, apart and together for over thirty years. We are still together (when I'm in town for HSN, I stay at 55 Plus Park, where Mike bought a place). I enjoy our Canadian neighbors, the statue of an old couple fishing next to a rare night blooming lotus in the front yard.

I didn't make a fuss. I accepted him as he was; I knew there was a meaning to being left alone on the huge farm. We would always be together, as side-by-siders.

Needing to be with loving pets and kisses on my face, I packed a bag and flew to my other home, my upstate New York mountain cabin where my two cats lived. (Ashley the mountain top neighbor is their stepmom when I am gone.)

The log cabin was under two feet of snow; the last blizzard had passed. The last snowstorm was the biggest of the year, just before spring. There was no road. I had to climb the hill with my tapestry luggage. Perfect!

Once inside, with my two cats for two weeks, I began to write and write and write. My phone was my only companion. Mary Alice Orito, my dearest friend called and said "Good, you're writing Book Two." I said, "I'm not writing Book Two, Book Two is writing me." Words are gushing out all over the computer screen.

I am now an old lady writing a book in bed!

Sassy, my beloved dog, on the Blackwater River, where I swim and meditate.

"You can always turn a bad kisser
into a good one."

LAURA PREPON

Always Turn the Bad Thing into a Good Thing

I turned the death of my dog Sassy, into Book Two, my book, *The Absolute Woman*.

With the farm house empty and all alone in the woods, with every single living thing gone, (except Mike's chickens), I began to write. I am not good at suffering. I can't suffer for more than three days. I need a motivation to move on and up, and stir my creative juices into an accomplishment. A bad thing can become that motivation.

I have been this way since I was a child, starting with my parent's divorce. Daddy left Mommy when I was three, which was unheard of in 1946. Grandma and Grandpa moved down from Hudson, NY, to the Washington apartment next door when I was five. I ate so well; I was always at their home, happy just devouring homemade blueberry pie à la mode. My mother was always on a grapefruit diet to weigh ninety-nine pounds, in case she was discovered to become a movie star. She was very beautiful, an artist and a dreamer.

I was an only child, always lonely, so my life's work was inviting other neighborhood kids to my home, to play and to entertain them. That's how I became the party girl and the sports fan. Now I could hang with all the cutest boys. "Mommy, can Jimmy come over and play? I'm all alone." "Yes," was always the guilty answer to the only child.

Bad things have been my life motivation. I almost wait for a bad thing to have the challenge of where it will take me. What's the reward for being a good girl in all the adversity? I turn up the dream machine in my brain and the message comes in loud and clear, COURAGE, VICKY, NOW YOU CAN DO THIS, PERMISSION GRANTED.

When I was not given the recommendations from my New York fashion college to get a job on Seventh Ave, my best friend Mia and I went to Paris and we opened our own company.

When Mia left me overnight, I didn't cry, I reopened my shop alone and became a brand.

When my marriage to a thirteen-year-older husband ended, I married a thirteen-year-younger husband.

When the expensive stores closed in the 2008 recession, I started selling on TV and started writing about my amazing, best-dressed movie star life.

My first divorce led me away from Hollywood/Paris to Florida/Paris, and a true country life with a country boy, Mike. I learned to grow food, eat fresh, and I gave up champagne and all meds, which led to a heathy life at seventy-five. I also learned to become comfortable friends with country folk who enabled me to work well on TV where I'm more relatable to an all-around audience, much more than the young girl who lived with Elizabeth Taylor. I also stopped crashing cars.

My children left Paris for crazy places and I became a mom alone, but our times together became a very special holiday.

My husband Mike had a love of leaving home and going off on fishing boats and oil rigs when farm life got him crazy, and I ended up meeting him in a lobster trailer somewhere for a make-up session when he called and missed me. As he is not a cheater, like my first husband, nor a gambler or a gangster, I'll take this behavior as his bad thing because mood swings are not on my No-No list. Having worked in movies and in fashion, mood swings come with the territory with many interesting, creative people, including my mom.

My advice on this most important life subject to you, my dear reader, is this:

MAKE A LIST OF YOUR WORST MOMENTS AND DRAW AN ARROW TO WHERE THEY LED YOU. WHEN THE NEXT HORRIBLE MOMENT ARRIVES, COUNT THE MOMENT AS A BLESSING AND IMAGINE THE GIFT, IMAGINE WHERE YOU ARE GOING, AND PROMISE YOURSELF TO GO THERE.

As they say in the Deep South, "If people give you lemons, always turn them into lemonade."

1. Life is Love ♥ ♥ ♥

2. Happiness and I Choose

3. Healthy Diet

4. Anger Management and Life is Love

5. Female Breadwinner

6. Staying Young and Beautiful Forever and Life is Love

Be The Absolute Woman

6 Search Phrase Verly Tiel

♥ ♥ ♥ ♥

*"To know yourself
is Enlightenment."*

MADELEINE VIONNET

It's All About Me and My Power

keep telling myself I'm middle aged, but I'm not. If this was the middle of my life I'd live to be 73 x 2, or 146. If I look at the math, 73 doesn't look like a middle age, but rather an "end of life" age, or just bloody OLD.

I can't be old! Look at me. I'm fit, curvy, and my hair is amazing. I just had sex with magic Mike and came nine times, a record for the two of us. Our "separation" was setting off sparks. Sometimes, walking down Park Ave, the Blvd Saint-Germain, or Heathrow Airport, some heads still turn, and not just women, to see what I'm wearing.

Of course, it helps to dress with great French style, with Ray-Bans to hide my eyes, Hermès scarves wrapped around me and my give-it-away neck. I'm covered in sparkling jewels on the chains of my diamond star necklace, and of course I'm wearing trendy, strappy booties. And yes, I'm old but forever fabulous. There is a new OLD today, a younger OLD, and I'm going to make the most of it.

On the road again, I got the Nashville hat before I knew my book publisher was located in Nashville. Life is magical.

"I didn't get there by wishing for it or hoping for it, but by working for it."

ESTÉE LAUDER

My Hot Babe Makeover

My Hot Babe Makeover for my first TV appearance on HSN started with a cab ride to New York City from our family's mountain cabin, above the Hudson River.

"Go slower," I screamed at the cab driver as he roared past yellow buses. "I'm a senior. I'm almost seventy." My long-haired driver who had a purple turban on his head turned to me and said, "You're not over fifty, Madame. Do not take me for a fool, just because I happen to be from India."

"It's my outfit that's young, I told him. I'm not," once again proving my point about men: It's all about the dress, or, how you dress is how men perceive you. I was wearing my new silver lamé tennis shoes with red patent heels, the absolute latest shoes in Paris, and a beaded T-shirt with an off-the-shoulder, black chiffon, see-thru peasant blouse over black stretch pants. He mistook me for a younger woman. It was a lovely gift to start my day.

I have always been reluctant to do plastic surgery and the puffy lip bit, or even the lightly tightened neck pull, as I tell my older show-biz friends who have all had it done, because I'm afraid to frighten my much younger husband off my body.

I am who he knows and I am still who he desires for the last thirty years. Surgery would be a possibility only if I needed a new man, so My Hot Babe Makeover must be limited to the outer me.

I lay in the chair of the handsome Central Park South dentist after hours of painless surgery, as Brian Kantor did perfect veneers on my front teeth. At last he finished and handed me a mirror. My yellow teeth (from a lifetime of drinking French espresso coffee every morning), were gone. Then the celebrity dentist told me, "You dressed my mom." I know I'm ancient, but the movie star's smile I had always dreamed of was there smiling back at me. Hello Pussycat! I had started the day looking fifty and now I was a hot forty and counting down.

I raced to Chinatown to the nail salon I frequent, after a late lunch of salmon and avocado sushi. While I ate, my nails were painted lilac with electric blue sparkles, making a new purple that shined like Day-Glo in the light. My ten-year-old granddaughter, Lucie Belle Berkeley, is the new colorist in the family and she told me that corals are over and purples are in at Target, where she is being taught fashion trends. She bought their entire Missoni collection when it came out, telling me that she bought two sizes of the larger zigzag sweaters to grow into, as they were timeless and would go with everything.

My last stop was the hairdresser, where Melba, who started life as an assistant to Kenneth (Jackie Kennedy's hairdresser), rules on the Upper East Side. Melba is the goddess of color. For three hours she streaked my hair with spiky silver points, turning me into a creature from a Tim Burton movie, into a glorious thirty-something, who raced out into the New York City streets singing the fun. song, "We Are Young."

see
thru
stretch jersey

black
jersey

as
a swimsuit

Vicky Tiel

"It is between you and God."

MOTHER THERESA

Being a Fashion Designer Is Not for the Sensitive

I am celebrating fifty-four years in fashion in 2018 and am today the longest lasting female designer in Paris. HOW? How did I last? By what miracle am I still sewing Vicky Tiel in the back of dresses?

It's quite simple. Being a fashion designer is not for the sensitive, heavy-hearted artist, confused into thinking that their egos are the labels in the back of a dress. Being a fashion designer is for the tough cookies, like my Mama said of me, "Vicky has no feelings, all she wants to do is play."

I really do have some feelings, but these feelings are mostly about food and sex and my feelings have pretty thick skin when it comes to fashion critiques. My brain has developed a pleasure-oriented life in France: sexual happiness with a good partner followed by a delicious, Mont Blanc hazelnut cream pastry is my idea of a day well spent.

My point of view about fashion is that I only want two things to happen: to sell and to sell, and if possible, to sell the exact same dress for thirty years—that works perfectly well for me. You see, lasting is all about selling, and selling dresses is all about LOOKING GOOD IN THE DRESS WHEN YOU ZIP IT UP. Fashion as pure art is great for a one-time show to make a name for yourself and crazy-shaped dresses are perfect to hang on museum walls under glass, but female humans have breasts, curves, and often short legs and fat arms, and the human eye is a nasty critic.

Fashion design is the toughest career for any of the artists (fine art, commercial art, music, acting), because you must have four collections a year (at least) and be judged at each show. The judges are journalists, merchants, your peers, and your customers. Fashion is the only one of all the arts where you have such exact dates you must "perform" up to eight times a year for the rest of your life, holidays included. No actor, singer, writer, painter, or dancer has such pressure, and that fact alone explains the crazy behavior of the fashion designers we have seen in the last thirty years.

Recently we saw the unexplainable death of the beautiful and talented L'Wren Scott, the girlfriend of Mick Jagger, and the fact that she hung herself on a piece of fabric is so fitting. She told the world that it was fashion that was too hard to handle, not the popstar boyfriend. You build yourself up to be Somebody, a Name, and failure and bankruptcy are not an option. In spite of having a wealthy backer, friends to network, and the press in love with you, plus a beautiful face and body to help promote your product, all the above does not help to sell enough product to be profitable, and most of the money you earn goes to becoming a famous brand and not to profit in your personal bank account.

In my first-year fashion class of Parsons 1961, there were forty students, and only sixteen graduated in 1964. Of the two award winners from our class, the one female student who teachers felt would make it to the top committed a young "suicide" after turning to drink (a fashion favorite), and our other student star (the next Yves Saint Laurent the school proclaimed) became the movie director Joel Schumacher. After only a year or two in the New York Seventh Ave dress world, Joel ran away in terror to Hollywood. We spoke years later at a party for Jack Nicholson, where a very laid-back Western-looking Joel asked me, "How can you do it?"

You have to have nerves of steel (or no feelings) to create a new look (short, sexy, thigh-high dresses), and to launch the look with partner Mia Fonssagrives in July 1964 Paris couture, and make the front page in the world press ("Mia and Vicky Conquer Paris"), only to have another designer married to a British public relations star claim she invented the mini. She invented the name, "The Mini," after a British car, but not the garment. Did I kill myself? No! I tell people today with a laugh, "I still sell dresses and Mary Quant sells nail polish."

In 1968, Mia and I made a sweet fitted dress that wrapped under the bust and tied around at the waist for the film *Candy*. We sold the dress to Bloomingdale's and the wrap dress appeared in *Redbook* magazine only to be "invented" in 1974 by a young designer, you all know who! Do I kill myself? No, I go to work and invent the "Pretty Woman" draped dress that is the longest selling gown in the history of the posh American department stores. It is celebrating forty years, even though it was copied for Julia Roberts after appearing in red in the window of Giorgio's of Beverly Hills Rodeo Drive. Still no suicide? No! Not likely. I would miss my favorite French pastry. Besides, I have sold thousands and thousands of "Pretty Woman" dresses at 4,000 dollars each. My acceptance of all things often gets a blessing. Oprah Winfrey was on the cover of her *Oprah* magazine in May 2014 wearing a long-sleeve "Pretty Woman" in purple, some twenty-four years after the film.

I had the rare opportunity to spend an evening with Coco Chanel (thanks to Elizabeth Taylor, it was my birthday present) in a "tête-à-tête" the year before she died. Coco at that point in her career had been thriving for over fifty years. She gave me the golden advice about lasting in fashion, which was to create and own a perfume that would represent me and sell forever, creating the brand. Coco was all business, down to earth, and exuding power as she proclaimed that great design is forever including her perfume bottle. Her cardigan jacket, quilted bag, and black-tipped beige shoe would be in every woman's wardrobe for half a century, yet Coco herself was not visible at chic parties, on TV talk shows, or lunching with Mme De Gaulle. If you wanted to meet Coco you had to fork out 10,000 dollars for a suit (in 1970) and she would measure you on Rue Cambon, and the Chanel suit would fit you perfectly. You would wear it forever and you would have met Madame.

"In the Final Analysis," as Mother Theresa proclaimed, "it's only between you and God," and in fashion, God is not Anna Wintour, but God instead transforms into the consumer, swiping a credit card with a good eye for what she looks like in the mirror when she puts on your work of art and proclaims, I LOVE IT!

I keep Mother Theresa's quote on my fridge.

Halle Berry

Cannes Film
Festival
2006

black jersey
and lace
corset dress

See thru legs

Vicky Tiel

"The man for me is the cherry on the pie. But I AM the pie and my pie is good all by itself. Even if I don't have a cherry."

HALLE BERRY

A Magical Miracle Just Happened to Me

A magical miracle happened to me, when a turquoise-blue ostrich feather fell from Heaven and landed on the doorstep of my upstate New York mountain cabin. I had been up in the log cabin alone for a week designing dresses and relaxing before my next HSN TV appearance. I was launching my first TV fragrance and had been told by their experts that selling something on TV that you can't smell is nearly impossible. That warning struck a worry chord, and I needed to ask for help.

I love the total quiet of a week alone in the log cabin, and now, each time before I go on TV, I sit in front of my mountaintop view of the Catskill Range and do a yoga meditation and feel the peace. I thank God for my blessings and sometimes ask for help.

This particular November morning was my last day at the cabin for the week. The skies were baby blue. The trees were all the colors of red, wine, and orange, and the leaves were falling into my hair as I sat on my chaise on the deck by the glass door. Some fear of failure passed through my mind and I prayed intensely and asked God to help me with my perfume launch. The perfume, 21 Rue Bonaparte, was named after my shop that I had opened with my partners Mia Fonssagrives and Elizabeth Taylor in the '60s.

I had worked in Paris since 1964 and in the late '80s Elizabeth and myself decided to do our own fragrances. We had been advised to do so in 1970 at a dinner with Coco Chanel just before her death. That night Coco gave us the best advice of our lives. Her greatest success, she told us, was the Chanel No. 5 perfume and it had self-financed her all her life. "Fashions and movies come and go, ladies, but a great fragrance is forever." We both followed her advice.

I set off in 1987 for Egypt, where perfume originated in 1000 BC. The word perfume derives from the Latin word meaning "through smoke," as the first perfumes were made in Cyprus by blending smoke with many natural aromatics and oils with water and alcohol. I copied the original bottle colors of the Queen of Egypt's amphors that I found at the Cairo Museum and took them back to the atelier of a Pierre Dinand, the French master bottle designer.

Now, after twenty perfumes, I would get to speak on TV to American ladies and explain **The Power of Femininity** and its relation to how we look and how we smell, as our perfume is our greatest memory.

I asked in my meditation, on the deck of the cabin, for the heavens to give me their blessings. After an hour or so I looked down only to find a miracle on the deck.

A BRILLIANT, 6-INCH-LONG, TURQUOISE-BLUE OSTRICH FEATHER LAY AT THE FRONT DOOR. IT HAD FALLEN FROM THE HEAVENS.

I picked it up and was amazed to find it, as there was no turquoise-blue bird ever in upstate New York. It seemed to be from a rare African bird or a dyed feather of a 1950s hat. Where had it come from? (I had designed a pink, ostrich-feather mini dress for Elizabeth Taylor to wear at a UNICEF gala.)

It was a magic miracle. I put the feather in my suitcase and decided to carry it with me forever, a sign from Elizabeth in heaven.

On the airplane to Tampa the next morning, with my eyes closed, soaring between the blue clouds, I realized that the feather was the exact same color as my first Egyptian perfume bottle. It was a message. It was a message from Elizabeth Taylor, who just recently went to heaven. She was telling me the perfume was going to be a big hit. She was right. I sold it out and I sell more perfume on TV than anyone.

Thank you, Elizabeth!

Elizabeth
Taylor's
Caftan

worn in
"Faustus"
Oxford
1965

Vicky
Tiel

*"God gave us the gift of life;
it is up to us to give ourselves
the gift of living well."*

VOLTAIRE

12 Lessons of Personal Power Taught to Me by the Powerful Women I've Dressed, from Brigitte Bardot to Kim Kardashian

1. Princess Grace taught me to dress in timeless fashion and in clothes that flatter you. Never wear ugly, ill-fitting clothes, like baggy T-shirts and big, sloppy shorts even if it's on the cover of *Vogue*.

2. Sophia Loren and Brigitte Bardot taught me that looking exciting in fab clothes to please your man is part of the sex act. It is not demeaning to wear my lacy "Priscilla Presley" bathrobe and spray the bedsheets with my Femme Absolute Perfume. Men need erections, women don't. Sophia and Brigitte also taught me that if you are confident you don't need to wear underwear. (Underwear also leaves an ugly mark on the backside of your pants.)

3. Lisa Fonssagrives Penn taught me to NOT BE AFRAID to tell your work partners, friends, and family how you feel about anything. Just tell them kindly, be lovely, and find the right moment.

4. Oprah Winfrey taught me to be generous and to truly love your friends and family. The more you have, the more you give. She lives to help others. One of the wealthiest families in Miami, the Holtz family, constantly throws charity lunches and sends thank you notes for everything. (After my book launch, they had my perfume bottle shape made into chocolates.) They live to give.

5. Elizabeth Taylor taught me that, "The person with the most money pays for lunch or dinner."

6. She also taught me that other than who pays for meals, everyone is equal. Being powerful is the opposite of being prejudiced. Elizabeth would seat her black, male "butler" next to Princess Margaret, or her French, karate-champ driver next to Princess Grace. This was the '60s. Never let anyone get away with being a snob.

7. Martha Stewart taught me that good work matters, so don't let anyone get away with a bad job. Compliment people who do a good job; give gifts to others for doing a great job. Martha also taught me to never give up, no matter what happens to you, and always be a lady.

8. My grandmother taught me young to never be afraid. If you see something wrong, speak out. (If I see children or animals being abused, I'll start screaming at the abusers to stop.) This is the only time I scream (outside of sporting events). I was at a local football game near my farm where an older couple was abusing a two-year-old who

wouldn't sit still. I screamed so much the school prin-
cipal came and the family left. I was the only one in the
stands to complain.

9. "Go for the man that loves you." This lesson was the
biggest shock, as I had never imagined that the most
beautiful women in the world don't go after men they
want. I have learned that men choose women for multiple reasons, but often they choose women they can
dominate. When women are deeply loved, there is nego-
tiation. My partner Elizabeth Taylor said, "Always go for
the man who loves you," and "Get the man who loves
you to buy you a gift of jewelry. Wear it all the time. It
reminds him that he LOVES YOU." I have a signature
charm necklace I always wear around my neck with
charms from all the men I've loved. My second husband
was so confident and full of himself, he never asked
me to take off the charms he didn't buy. (Of course, he
was thirty years younger than the first husband, so that
helped!) A great lesson from Elizabeth that I see Kim
Kardashian has taken to heart.

10. Never judge a book by its cover. When the third richest
woman in the world, Miriam (Mrs. Sheldon Adelson),
came into Bergdorf, no one recognized her in her gray
sweats and tennis shoes with two heavyset, thug-like
men. No designer would talk to her. I walked over and
sold her a gown that she wore to the opening of her
casino in Manila. Shirlee Fonda (Mrs. Henry Fonda)
walked into Neiman Marcus Beverly Hills in 1982
wearing a black and white stretch gym outfit! The first
anyone had ever seen, but today all Planet Earth wears
the Fonda gym look that made everyone's mouth open.

11. Ursula Andress taught me to know your best feature and show it. (Her legs.)
12. Goldie Hawn taught me to laugh every day and always have fun. She also taught the world that a marriage license doesn't matter.

Famous Women Leaders (and Positive Examples) Empowering Women Everywhere

* Katherine Hepburn—introduced the world to modern cinema
* Eleanor Roosevelt—early advocate of women's rights and racial equality
* Margaret Thatcher—"The Iron Lady" led conservative England into modern times
* Margaret Sanger—advocate for birth control; opened first clinic for birth control in the United States
* Simone de Beauvoir—writer, existentialist, philosopher, early feminist, and political activist
* Françoise Sagan—novelist and screenwriter, most famous for her first book, *Bonjour Tristesse*
* Gloria Steinem—feminist journalist who led the American feminist movement in the late 1960s
* Aretha Franklin—first female artist inducted into the Rock and Roll Hall of Fame

* Jeanne Moreau—French actress, star of *Jules et Jim*, where she provoked two men who loved her to fight over her
* Sophia Loren—Italian actress who rose from poverty to be the first to win an Oscar for a foreign-language film
* Elizabeth Taylor—actress, promoted racial and LGBT equality, AIDS awareness, and was the first woman to earn one million dollars for a movie
* Betty Friedan—author of *The Feminine Mystique* who brought second wave feminism in the early '60s
* Indira Gandhi—first, and only, female Prime Minister of India
* Estée Lauder—founder, chief developer of international cosmetics company
* Golda Meir—Israeli Prime Minister and political figure of importance
* Sandra Day O'Connor—first woman selected to serve on the United States Supreme Court
* Rosa Parks—symbol of equality and known as mother of the modern day American civil rights movement
* Helena Rubinstein—Polish-American businesswoman who founded a cosmetics company, art collector and philanthropist
* Taylor Swift—Grammy-award-winning singer/songwriter who sings about her life experiences
* Mother Theresa—Nobel Prize winner, founder of Missionaries of Charity to help those suffering from poverty
* Marguerite Duras—novelist, playwright, and filmmaker of human sexuality

* Elizabeth Arden—marched for women's rights (supplied the red lipstick for 15,000 marchers) who took cosmetics mainstream and her brand worldwide
* Rachel Carson—author of *Silent Spring*, which launched the global environmental movement
* Coco Chanel—started her own company and created timeless fashion (jersey, sportswear) and perfume
* Empress Dowager Cixi—helped bring China into the modern world
* Julia Child—senior civilian intelligence officer for the OSS during World War II, author and television star who brought French cuisine to American households
* Marie Curie—winner of two Nobel Prizes (Physics and Chemistry), discovered radium and polonium
* Miley Cyrus—modern child star with a purpose
* Yoko Ono—artist, singer, songwriter, peace activist, and artistic inspiration for John Lennon
* Princess Diana—refused to say "I will obey" when she married Prince Charles
* Angela Merkel—first female Chancellor of Germany, took in displaced Arabs
* Oprah Winfrey—leader in media, perfect example of Feminine Power today
* Malala Yousafzai—symbol of Arab female equality, shot and survived at age twelve
* Krista Suh and Jayna Zweiman of Pussyhat Project—lately started the inevitable vibes in women that lead to the #MeToo movement
* Diane Nash—created the Freedom Riders with Martin Luther King, Jr.

Kim
Kardashian

2009

Vicky Tiel

Quotes I Love!

"Create the life you want with six things:
presence, authenticity, sensuality, spirituality,
gratitude, and always be kind."
KATHE GREEN

"I avoid looking back, I prefer good memories to regrets."
GRACE KELLY

"Your dresses should be tight enough to show you're a
woman and loose enough to show you're a lady."
EDITH HEAD

"Love yourself more."
LINDA DRESNER

"Everybody must embrace the next thing in front of them.
We don't get to coast through life, we must embrace
the change, especially our jobs."
MARY ALICE ORITO

The Absolute Woman

"God is a *fucking woman!*"
ANI BERKELEY, MY DAUGHTER-IN-LAW

"Nothing makes a woman more beautiful
than the belief that she is beautiful."
SOPHIA LOREN

"I shall die very young. Maybe sixty, maybe seventy,
maybe eighty...but I shall be very young."
JEANNE MOREAU

"Fashion is a powerful tool. It is not superficial.
Why does it matter? Your clothes are the first thing people
see when they look at you. Even before you open your
mouth, what you wear speaks volumes about who you are
and how you are perceived. Like it or not, first impressions
matter. Clothing is the outward manifestation of YOU!"
MARILYN KIRSCHNER

I keep Sister Theresa's quote on my fridge.

The Final Analysis

People are often unreasonable, illogical, and self centered;
Forgive them anyway.

If you are kind, people accuse you of selfish, ulterior motives;
Be kind anyway.

Be Here Now

If you are successful, you will win some false friends and some true enemies;
Succeed anyway.

If you are honest and frank, people may cheat you;
Be honest and frank anyway.

What you spend years building, someone may destroy overnight;
Build anyway.

If you find serenity and happiness, they may be jealous;
Be happy anyway.

The good you do today, people will often forget tomorrow;
Do good anyway.

Give the world the best you have, it may never be enough;
Give the world the best you've got anyway.

You see, in the Final Analysis, it is all between you and God;
It was never between you and them anyway.

My Mantra

Books on My Porch, on My Swing, and by My Bed

A Walk Across America by Peter Jenkins

How Successful Artists Study by Samuel Adoquei

The Heart Is A Lonely Hunter by Carson McCullers

The Art of War by Sun Tzu

The Accidental Feminist by M. G. Lord

Unmitigated Gaul by Suzanne White

The Power of Now by Eckhart Tolle

The Culture of Narcissism by Christopher Lasch

The Tibetan Yogas of Dream and Sleep by Tenzin Wangyal Rinpoche

My Lord Loves a Pure Heart by Swami Chidvilasananda

The Life of Birds by David Attenborough

Vicky Tiel

Physical Anthropology and Archeology by Clifford J. Jolly and Fred Plog

Inside Animal Minds by National Geographic

The Untethered Soul by Michael A. Singer

Family of Earth and Sky by John Elder and Hertha D. Wong

Mademoiselle: Coco Chanel and the Pulse of History by Rhonda K. Garelick

Food, Health, and Happiness by Oprah Winfrey

My favorite photo for Vogue ads. Makeup and hair by my husband Ron, who also shot me better than anyone.